THE LANGUAGE LENS FOR CONTENT CLASSROOMS

A GUIDEBOOK FOR TEACHERS, COACHES & LEADERS

2ND EDITION

SARAH B OTTOW

Second Edition. May 2023.
ISBN: 978-1-961397-00-2

Publisher: Confianza LLC
www.ellconfianza.com

AUTHOR'S NOTE

~

Many teachers, coaches and leaders come to me, perplexed about how to support language in the classroom for multilingual and multicultural students of any age. It is all too easy to feel overwhelmed and underconfident. However, the last thing we need is more overwhelmed educators!

I believe that any educator can support any learner with the right tools and confidence in themselves, building on their strengths. I wrote this book for the countless educators I'm so fortunate to work with every day. This book is designed to *demystify* language learning for all educators. Let's work towards a shared knowledge base and a shared mission to welcome, nurture and teach all students so that they can reach their potential.

I also wrote this book for my younger, less experienced self. This is the book I wish I had when I started out as a general education classroom teacher. I would have greatly benefited from the tips and reminders to support my diverse classroom. Later in my career, as a language specialist and as a literacy/instructional coach, this guide would have been very useful to ground me for validation of what I was trying to do. I also would have referred to this book for ideas of how I could support other educators as an instructional leader.

Most of all, I wrote this book for my students. Throughout my career as an educator in the US and internationally, I've been lucky to work with students and families from over 40 language groups. What I have learned from my students is immeasurable. What I have yet to learn is humbling.

As you'll discover in this guidebook, the Language Lens® is an established approach and a framework I developed through my work leading my organization, Confianza. I'm excited to share it with you. Please visit languagelens.com for more resources and to stay connected on our social channels.

Thank you to my family, my team at Confianza, and a special thank you to my editor of this second edition, Fatima Hassan.

Sarah Bernadette Ottow

CONTENTS

CHAPTER 1
STARTING WITH THE END IN MIND

WELCOME TO OUR JOURNEY OF TEACHING, LEARNING AND LEADING WITH A *language lens*®! I am very excited about guiding you on this adventure dedicated to the students in your classroom (if you are a teacher) or your school (if you are a coach or school leader). In this guide designed for educators from all grade levels, ages and subject areas, I will show you how to create your personalized professional learning map for supporting language learners--MLLs and ALLs. In this guidebook, I will be guiding you through a set of mindsets and practices that can be applied universally for any age student in any school. Your job will be to discern what *you* need and what *your students* need so that you can then transfer these mindsets and practices to your unique setting. You will see that this is not an entirely new approach but, instead, a way of looking at planning, teaching and assessing more intentionally. I will bring in practical tips and tools along the way to support you and help you check for understanding so that you and all your students can get to the learning destination we have planned for them. The big goal here is to remove barriers to learning and *loving* to learn—both for students and their educators. As you move through this guidebook, I urge you to look within to see how much you are already likely doing while gleaning some little ways to improve your teaching and learning in big ways!

In this introductory chapter, I will set the scene, so to speak, about why a language lens is a difference-maker for ALL students and share ways to get started. In this chapter and all subsequent chapters, you see *essential questions* listed for two potential groups of educators interacting with this guidebook. Here are Chapter 1's questions for you to consider:

- Essential Question for ALL Educators, Especially Teachers: How Do We Get Started with Developing Our Language Lens?
- Essential Question for Coaches/Leaders: How Can We Ensure High Expectations That Positively Impact Our Professional Learning Culture?

This guide was designed for educators of two types of students:

1. English language learners (ELLs)/Multilingual learners (MLLs)
2. Academic language learners (ALLs)

First, for those of you who teach English language learners, also known as MLLs, English learners (ELs), Multilingual Learners (MLLs), emerging bilinguals, and perhaps other terms used to describe this group of learners in your local area. In this guidebook, I will use the term MLL. A Multilingual Learner is a student who is acquiring English as a second or (sometimes third, fourth, or fifth!) additional language. You may already know that, as a very diverse subgroup of various linguistic and cultural backgrounds, MLLs are the fastest-growing population of students in U.S. schools. It is estimated that by 2025, an average of one in four students in any given U.S. classroom will be an MLL student. Multilingual learners are doing double-duty since they have to learn both the content *and* the English language. While many MLLs are U.S.-born, it's also interesting to note that our nation's immigration population has doubled since 1990 (PEW, 2014; U.S. Department of Education, 2018). Multilingual learners are extremely diverse, speaking more than 400 languages, learning two or several languages, and attending all kinds of school districts--urban, suburban, exurban, and rural (NCES, 2020). Students experiencing homelessness, students in Title I (free and reduced lunch status) and migrant students have been more likely to be categorized as students learning English than other students in U.S. schools (U.S. Department of Education, 2018).

Miguel Cardona, the U.S. Secretary of Education, says that bilingual and bicultural identities are "as American as apple pie" (para. 4, Turner, 2021). Like myself, Secretary Cardona is the first in his family to graduate from college, and he advocates for those who are the most vulnerable in our schools. Furthermore, Cardona has called for U.S. schools to now view students who know more than one language as having superpowers in the global workforce, promoting funding for dual language programs and pushing for all students to learn more than just English. There are so many advantages to having a bilingual/multilingual brain, yet in the United States, almost 80% of its residents speak primarily English (Commission on Language Learning at the American Academy of Arts and Sciences, n.d.). Cardona's message flips the view that students learning English have a deficit and shouldn't be allowed to speak other languages in school. Unfortunately, this narrow concept is illustrated by years of restrictive language policies in the U.S. (Canto, 2023). However, Cardona's global and equity-based perspective coming from the very top of public education is precisely what we need right now. It's what we have always needed, and it's what this book promotes.

Bridging the Opportunity Gap

A reason why you're likely reading this book is that most general education teachers and coaches/leaders who support them have not been adequately trained or supported to effectively reach and teach MLLs (National Council on Teacher Quality, 2015; English Learner Success Forum, 2022). Historically, MLL students have largely been either placed in sink-or-swim programs or remedial-type programs that don't meet their needs. MLL students have experienced an *opportunity gap* of not having more qualified educators teach them both content and language in their general education classroom or at the

Tier 1 level. What do I mean when I say *opportunity gap*? An opportunity gap can be viewed as factors outside of a student's control like financial insecurity and systemic inequities. However, in my view, because many of our MLL students don't have access to highly qualified teachers, coaches, and leaders, this student group experiences an opportunity gap of underqualified educators that we must address immediately and in an ongoing way.

Having multilingual students in our population is not a problem to be solved but an opportunity to seize. Students from outside the dominant culture and language of school often face a *system*—not just individual classrooms—that is not necessarily designed with their diversity and with an inclusive vision in mind. Along with this vision comes specific skills for teaching, coaching, and leading with a language lens. I believe that as educators and as a *system*, it's well past time to center the assets and needs of our most diverse students as we design relevant, rigorous, and joyful schools! As a system, we should refrain from problematizing the presence of diverse students. We should move away from deficit-based thinking and behavior, towards more asset-based thinking and behavior, and, better yet, as I will explain in this book, more *equity-based* thinking and behavior. Instead of *admiring the problem,* I ask you not to see diversity as a problem but as a beautiful and important opportunity to improve schooling for ALL of us. Instead of seeing low achievement as a *within child issue,* I invite you to step back and see it as a *within system issue.* That's what this journey into the language lens is all about.

As an equity-focused consultant and professional development specialist, I begin working with a school by asking about their vision of equitable instruction. Every school needs a cohesive vision of effective instruction for MLLs that helps general educators—or, as I will refer to in this book, content teachers—to also support the MLLs in their classroom (Gee, 2008; Quintero & Hansen, 2017). We start with the end in mind by envisioning equity for ALL of our students. Even if your MLL students work primarily with an MLL specialist—or, as I will refer to in this book, a *language specialist*—if you are a content teacher, it is critical to help students access the content in your classroom. It is not enough to have language instruction as an add-on or a separate service where only the language specialist attends to language; instead, we need all teachers to develop a language lens. This means we need language to be more explicit and attended to in not just core classrooms (English language arts, math, science, social studies) but also in every discipline across a school (arts, technology, music, consumer education, etc.). The vision of equitable instruction should include easy-to-understand look-fors that promote shared responsibility from all educators to reach and teach all students.

If you are reading this book as a coach and leader, your role is to create and sustain this vision of equitable instruction for your school throughout this book, starting with the questions and tips later in this introductory chapter and presented throughout this book at the end of each chapter. Your role is to support teachers and guide them under shared language and shared tools for your school. Your role is to help shift the culture and climate towards inclusivity. Your role is to plant seeds for positive change across the system and, when the seeds bloom, showcase the harvest for others to learn from. Overall, as an instructional leader, your greatest power is in "choosing the narrative" for your school community where trust is evident and students can become their own teachers (p. 73, Hattie, 2023).

We need to keep in mind that much of the way we teach, coach and/or lead is based on how we learned, and many of us may not have been multilingual students or multilingual citizens of the world ourselves. In many respects, the systems we operate within in schools are outdated and do not necessarily serve the diversity of the students of the here and now. You see, as educators, we are products of the very system we are trying to change from within. That's why we must back up and see the big picture of who schools were originally designed for and ask ourselves, *Are our schools, our classrooms set up for ALL of my students to succeed? Are we inspiring ALL students to learn, pursue their passions, and be their authentic selves? How can we learn from those on the margins so that all students' needs are centered, not just those student groups who have been historically successful in U.S. school systems?*

My passion for bringing the language lens to classrooms and instructional leaders has driven me since I began teaching over twenty years ago. In fact, after fifteen years of teaching and coaching within school systems, universities, and adult literacy centers, I started an organization, Confianza, to advance equity, language, and literacy for MLLs and ALL students. In my daily practice, I teach, coach, train, and consult with content and language teachers, teacher leaders, coaches, principals, and directors. My team at Confianza creates and curates content based on evidence-based practices that builds capacity to reach and teach language learners in schools, *all* language learners. You see, there is power in fostering metacognition (thinking about thinking) and metalinguistic awareness (thinking about language). This book provides an introductory set of resources from Confianza to facilitate your learning. It is designed as a starting point for self-study or team-based professional development.

This guidebook aims to put a vision of effective instruction into an operational set of practices for any teacher of MLL students. This brings me to the second type of student this guide was designed to help.

Academic Language Learners in Every Content Classroom

Throughout this guide, I will call academic language learners ALLs. An ALL is any student who is learning academic language. Jeff Zwiers (2014), a key scholar in the field of academic language, defines academic language as "the set of words, grammar, and discourse strategies used to describe complex ideas, higher-order thinking processes, and abstract concepts" (p. 22). Academic language learning happens in every classroom no matter where we teach—elementary school, middle school, high school, and adult learning spaces. Academic language learning is happening in *what* we teach--math, language arts, science, social studies, the arts, technology, consumer education, or any content area. This means that any student in your class is engaging in learning the academic language. This also means that, as adult learners, we are also learning language in any given context! More than anything, this fact of language being a part of any classroom means that all teachers need to engage language learners in using language meaningfully within their own disciplines (Heritage, Walqui, & Linquanti, 2015).

You might be thinking, *An academic language learner . . . doesn't that mean virtually any student I have?* And the answer is yes. Any student at any time is learning not just content but the academic language of the content we are teaching! Yes, we are all teaching language. We cannot teach our content without it!

Please be aware that academic language does not necessarily come easily to any student, English learner or not. You see, all students need to learn not just the *content* but the nuanced *language* needed to process and apply the content standards, skills, and knowledge. As I will explain in this guide, the discourse of academic language is what school is all about and is what higher education and the professional fields expect. Having a command of context-appropriate academic language—in terms of both *quality* and *quantity* of language--is what we aim for when we talk about students being *college and career ready*. I prefer to add *life ready* as well, since there's more to the goal of education than college and career. We want our students to be ready for any challenge and choice in their path- or college, career, and life ready- so that they can comprehend information and express themselves fluently. Language is a vehicle for success. We all need a language lens as content teachers, and if you are a coach or leader, you need a language lens as well to support both educators and students within your school's diverse learning spaces.

The Role of the Educator in Cultural and Linguistic Communication

There is an implicit set of expectations around academic language that may not always be clear for both teachers and students alike. In other words, much of the language needed to be successful is cultural and largely invisible. For example, as the oldest sibling in my family, a first-generation college graduate and former free-and-reduced lunch student, there was a lot about navigating high school and college that was completely new to me. Terms like *honors courses, FAFSA, and work-study* seemed like a new language that I was supposed to know to get on the right pathway after high school graduation.

In 10th grade, I moved across the country from Cape Cod, Massachusetts, to Southcentral Wisconsin. As I stepped into the Midwestern culture and dialect, terms like *bubbler* and *tennis shoes* were confusing, never mind ending questions with prepositions, like, *Want to come with?* It all felt and sounded so strange. I left field hockey behind on the East Coast to join a new sport, track, in Wisconsin. When we were learning how to sprint the 200-meter race more efficiently, my coach explained that we should maximize the power from our arms as they moved opposite the legs as we sprinted. He explained that we needed to bring each arm all the way up, almost next to our shoulder, and then all the way back behind us very quickly. To make his point, the coach said, *Cow, wall. Cow, wall,* as he moved his hands back and forth purposefully. My teammates nodded in recognition while I stood there, puzzled. *Cow, wall?! What is happening here? I thought we were learning how to sprint. Why are we talking about cows and walls?* I found the courage to ask the coach what he meant by cow, wall. My teammates laughed, *Milking a cow! You don't know how to milk a cow?!* The coach broke it down for me; w*hen you milk a cow, your hand goes up to the cow's udder and then straight back behind you, toward the wall. That's how I want your arms to move when you're running fast.* You see, I had no background knowledge for this language nor this gesture. Suffice to say, to this day, I always think of milking a cow when I go for a run, even though I have yet to ever actually milk a cow in my life!

As this example shows you, not only is language so enmeshed in culture, language can *include* and it can also *exclude* learners. For groups who do not speak the "standard" target language at home and those learning an additional language from a home language or languages other than English, we need to be careful not to assume they have the same linguistic and cultural perspective! We also need to ensure that all groups feel welcome at school and that those from other language groups see their language as just as valid as the dominant discourse. I even question terms like *non-standard* to describe linguistic groups like African American English (AAE), for example, because what is *standard* anyways? We are humans from all backgrounds and experiences. While our schools and the larger society may impart *a dominant culture and dominant language,* it is our job as educators to make sure every learner is able to exert agency over their own learning experience and see their culture and language background mirrored in the school, not as *non-dominant* or *less than*. We all matter and we should all feel like we belong within a learning community.

Thus, language and culture matter, and they are intimately connected. That's why we need to be aware of what academic language is, the power it has over school success, and the key it can be to post-K–12 choices. As Jeff Zwiers (2014) concludes, not only is academic language "much more complex and important than most educators realize" (p. xi), it is:

1. Intricately linked to higher-order thinking processes
2. Developed by extensive modeling and scaffolding of classroom talk
3. Accelerated by weaving in direct teaching of its features while teaching concepts of a content area

All this to say, as educators we have tremendous power to help or hinder our students' love of learning!

Educators as Agents of Socialization

As educators, we are each in a huge position of power over our students in our role. Educators are *agents of socialization* because we don't just communicate language and content, we also reinforce—or interrupt—the values and beliefs of our cultural communities (Adger, Snow, & Christian, 2018). We need to go beyond being dispensers of knowledge to students who may be perceived as vessels being filled with the knowledge we provide. To ensure that students are engaged in the learning process and make sense of what they are learning in ways that are meaningful to them, we must shift towards co-constructing knowledge with our students. Recognizing our students' backgrounds and identities, as well as those of their families, is crucial in creating learning experiences that validate their cultural heritage while also teaching them academic expectations. In this way, we can learn from our students as we teach them.

In this journey together, I'd like to share with you how your role can be more culturally and linguistically responsive and sustaining through developing your own language lens. As you'll learn in our adventure together, the language lens is an approach I developed throughout my career and have operationalized in our professional learning services at Confianza. The book aims to be an introduction and overview of how to use a language lens in your classroom, or for those of you who coach or lead, in your work supporting other educators.

The Language Lens

My experience has taught me that if we look through the language lens, we center the needs of our linguistically diverse students. Subsequently, we not only improve our mindsets and practices for that subgroup of students but we improve our entire approach for teaching and learning for ALL of our students. This is not to say that our multilingual students do not require additional support and accommodations. They do, and that's why it is important to work collaboratively to support students individually, especially with your language specialist. However, if we think of improving general education classrooms' Tier 1 or universal instruction, we improve accessibility for ALL of our students. With this language lens approach, we are making the achievement of all students a *general education issue,* not just an issue for the MLL department to tackle. We are also seeing the promise, the strength, and the beauty that diversity brings. As a person who grew up close to the ocean, I like to say, *A high tide lifts all boats.* If we center the experiences of our linguistically diverse students as we plan, teach, and assess, we can become more equitable educators for all of our students! This is the goal of the language lens—investing in all students' identities and boosting the learning of all of our students through speaking, listening, reading, and writing skills. We can support all students in their academic success and, ultimately, their career, college, workplace, and life readiness!

Who This Guide Is For

Whether you are a language specialist or a content specialist, if you have students with English language needs or students with any language or literacy need, or if you are a coach or leader supporting other educators with these needs, my hope is that you will get some practical guidance from this book for developing a language lens in your daily practice. While designed with the U.S. K–12 classroom in mind, educators working in adult educator or international private schools can benefit as well. However, if you fall in this category, you'll need to think about the content standards differently depending on the curricular framework you use (i.e., International Baccalaureate). Since 2015, I have used this language lens approach in schools and districts across over 30 U.S. states and several countries through my coaching, training, consulting, and Confianza's online course offerings.

This book provides an overview of the language lens for educators looking for some key takeaways to advance their practice by infusing more linguistic and cultural awareness and integration in their teaching, coaching, or leading. If you're looking for more in-depth resources, head over to languagelens.com. You'll see featured tools from this guidebook available for free download, plus collections of additional resources organized in the following six categories:

1. Curriculum and Instruction
2. Data and Assessments
3. Dual Language and Biliteracy
4. Family and Student Engagement
5. Leading for Equity
6. Professional Learning and Collaboration

If you are a general educator of students of any age but do not currently have any multilingual students, you will also get ideas from this guide. After all, your students are tasked with learning the academic language of your content area. But if you have both MLLs and ALLs, you will significantly benefit from this book because that is who the book especially addresses. In my work supporting K–12 schools and educators from every content area across the United States and internationally, I see classrooms full of various language needs and, as I said earlier, not so much training for teachers in a sink-or-swim situation themselves! Offering minimal or no special support to MLLs is not only ineffective, it is also illegal under United States legislation from the Office for Civil Rights (Krashen & Crawford, 2015).

Education is a civil right, and for historically marginalized populations, we need to continuously attend to these rights so that we don't (unintentionally) perpetuate inequities of the past. In fact, to me, striving towards equity means intentionally centering those who have historically been on the margins in our learning spaces, including all families and caregivers. I find that leaving educators on their own to inadequately meet the needs of increasingly diverse student populations in their classrooms isn't equitable either. We need to build *collective efficacy* where every educator in a school sees their impact "first through the impact on those needing greatest growth and scale" (Hattie, 2023, p. 422). On this journey, I aim to offer a support system for you as you navigate the diverse needs and strengths of your students, and strive to plan, teach, and assess with language in mind for any content area you may be teaching or supporting. This lifeboat of support is intended to help you become more efficient and effective in your instructional practices, leveraging your own strengths in this process.

Language specialists are also encouraged to read this guide alongside their content teacher colleagues to find *entry points* or ways to collaborate for students' benefit. Don't forget, any space you teach in has its own language as well, including English Language Development (ELD) class! The role of the specialist exists for a reason; you have expertise. When I was a language specialist, I felt like every teacher should know what I knew! I didn't have any magic dust that suddenly taught students how to be fully proficient in English, as many of my colleagues seemed to have inferred, asking me to *fix this child*. There was nothing to fix within the child, only within the classroom. Those years *in the trenches* helped me see that I can't change the system single-handedly, but I can help one teacher at a time, collaborating for the benefit of our shared students. I could focus on what was directly within my *sphere of influence.*

While this book is primarily geared towards educators who *don't* currently see themselves as educators of language, if you are a language specialist, this book can help you, too. If you are in a teacher leadership role, you may want to read both sections at the end of each chapter—the section for teachers and the section for coaches and leaders. Many language specialists are in a middle space, navigating between being a teacher and being, what I like to call, a *leader-with-a-lower-case-l.* In other words, you're not a *leader-with-an-upper-case-L,* like an administrator, yet you find yourself supporting teachers constantly as a *de facto teacher leader,* whether you signed up for that part of the job or not. Believe me, I've been there and see it all the time in my work today. Much of the system's change you seek for students may be outside of your direct influence, yet perhaps in this book, you can uncover ways to transfer learnings to your role as an agent of change in your school. Check out resources for professional learning and collaboration at languagelens.com, too!

If you're a school leader or instructional coach, I'll encourage you to embed the information from this guidebook right into your professional learning culture in a sustaining way. I'll pose questions to you after you have digested each chapter so that you can take what you need, what your educators need, and what your school community needs for *just in time* learning. If you are designing professional learning based on this book or referring to this book, please keep in mind the following:

1. Learn from teachers as you design and redesign your professional learning. Teachers prefer professional learning experiences that are job-embedded, solution-oriented, teacher-led, personalized/differentiated, compensated, and considerate of emotional and mental health (p. 3, Durham, 2023). I myself am a massive fan of mapping out a year-long professional learning cycle with varied opportunities for teachers to learn together and from one another. As a professional learning specialist, my role is to coach the leadership team, provide field-tested resources and co-create a potential road map for student-centered, teacher-driven change. This guidebook lays out a potential map to do so!

2. If you're looking for more support or ideas, stay connected with me and my organization, Confianza, for related professional learning workbooks and tools that may help you in your quest. As previously

mentioned, resources directly related to this guidebook can easily be found at languagelens.com. You can also find me directly at sarahottow.com and on the social channels listed there.

The Second Edition

The first edition of *The Language Lens for Content Classrooms* guidebook was published in 2019. This is the second edition of this book, and I'm excited to share what's new about it. First, because I believe that it takes a village to enact systems change, I have included special guidance for coaches and leaders within each chapter. I use this guidance in my consulting with my coach and leader clients, so I hope it's useful for you, too, dear reader. Coaches and leaders can lead by example, model effective practices, and nudge others to improve all for the benefit of the shared learners in your unique community. Second, I have brought in updated resources from the field. For further study, check out the resources mentioned throughout that go into more depth than is covered in this book, all available at languagelens.com. Last but definitely not least, in this edition, I discuss implications from some of the lessons learned due to schools having gone through the COVID-19 pandemic and the underlying inequities the pandemic exposed further. For example, the pre-existing and long-standing teacher shortage was unfortunately exacerbated by the COVID-19 pandemic, especially in schools serving students of color and students from low-income households, where teachers are recruited to work with low wage and high stress (Schmitt & DeCourcy, 2022).

Inquiry as Personalized Professional Learning

Because this guide is meant as a survey of sorts for all educators of students of any age, I present general yet universal information that you can tailor to your specific context and your students. You'll see lots of ideas and suggestions, which is to say that you do not need to integrate every idea I share! It's up to you to take what I share and consider whether it's relevant or viable for your situation, your school, and your students. Sure, I may be bringing expertise to this guide on supporting diversity and inclusion through this equity-based lens, but you are bringing expertise in your own content area, your own students, and your own learning community. Transfer and adapt what I present as needed to your own situation.

Practical professional development is very important to me, and in my everyday work, I try to ensure that the educators I train and coach have what they need to apply a mindset to their practice that immediately supports their students. In this guide, I will be relying on you to continually reflect on what is already working for you, what could work for you, and of course, what you'll commit to trying out! We know that just like the most effective professional development is not just *sit-and-get*, the most effective educators are intrinsically reflective, constantly thinking, *What can I do better next time? How can I transfer this great idea into my classroom?* This is what we call inquiry (Ottow & Holmes, 2015).

As educators, we can improve our practice by learning from research by university professors, and we can also conduct our own research in our schools and classrooms. In fact, practitioner research on practice within our settings is more likely to improve our practice than relying on university-level research. It is also more engaging and actually "democratized research" (p. 139, Cochran-Smith and Lytle, 2009). As practitioners leading our own inquiry cycles in our classrooms, we are essentially conducting ongoing action research. We are continuously adjusting our practice to address students' needs.

As you work with this guidebook, choose one or two things to try out in the spirit of inquiry, not a laundry list of new strategies all at once! Taking on too much at once can set us up to fail, and we will never be able to try out a new tip with integrity or intention. So please, take this opportunity to think critically about your practice, refresh yourself on what you need, and, most importantly, focus on what your students need to have meaningful learning experiences in your classroom. Throughout the guide, I'll be reminding you to continually reflect and consider next steps, whether engaging in this professional learning on your own or in a team. I strongly encourage teams to work together, with the guidance of a coach and/or school leader, but if that's not available, the guidebook is also set up for individual self-study.

Whether you're reading this book solo or with a team, I encourage you to consider what ideas you can take back to your classroom, team, or school *right away*. You'll engage in a self-assessment at the end of this first chapter that can help you focus on what *you* need for *your students*. Think of this book as personalized professional learning! As I like to say, professional learning is an ongoing *habit of mind,* not just a one-and-done event! Come back to the book for more as needed, or use the topics presented in the text as a take-off point for more learning on your professional learning path.

Many teachers I work with use the guidebook as a reference to choose one or more practices to try out and then come back to the book later to try out something else. Others use ideas presented in the book to help create their SMART goals for the school year, aligned with their students' needs. Some teacher education programs provide this text to teachers learning how to teach or adding on an additional license. You'll also see some information at the end of this chapter about a companion process for professional learning called Confianza's Action Cycle®. However, you found this book, and however you plan to utilize it, welcome!

Collaboration = Co + Laboring

Some of you may be reading this on your own. Some of you may be lucky enough to work together. When content teachers and language specialists collaborate in planning, teaching, and assessing, the responsibility becomes shared. In my work, I see more and more schools moving towards more intentional teaming, professional learning communities, collaborative planning time, and co-teaching instructional models. For our multilingual learners, co-teaching can reduce the isolation teachers often experience without taking away the autonomy needed to meet various students' needs (Honigsfeld and Dove, 2019).

Language can be the bridge to bring content teachers and language specialists together for student success. We want the language lens to be part of every educator's approach, not just the language specialist's. As you'll unpack with me throughout this guide, language is part of every learning environment, and when we view what we teach through the language lens, we can demystify *what* students are learning and *how* they are learning it!

If you can trust the process with me, let the journey begin!

Beginning our Language Lens Journey

As we move through this guide, I will be sharing ways you can develop your language lens for what both MLLs and ALLs need to access the content of your classroom. As you get started, please note a few things. First, depending on the individual student, multilingual learners often require additional scaffolding and cultural considerations, which are typically under the purview of the language specialist, so please collaborate and make sure that individual students get what accommodations they are entitled to within the general education classroom and also outside of it if they have separate instruction with the language specialist.

Please keep in mind that the language lens is *not an add-on.* The language lens is an *approach,* a new way of thinking about teaching and learning for all educators. Yet, as many of my clients discover, it's not so new after all! You may find you already think of a lot of the concepts and practices shared in this book which will hopefully be wonderfully validating for you! You may also find that much of the information is completely new to you and will hopefully be remarkably useful! It all depends on your unique experience as an educator and as a unique individual in the world outside of school.

Having a language lens means that we need to develop a way to think about and operationalize the academic language of our content through which to plan, teach, and assess. When I refer to academic language throughout the book, I will also point out that culture is an inherent aspect of language since language and content cannot really be separated. People interact with language differently across different contexts and cultures; nothing is wrong with being different. In this book, we will widen our aperture to get to know our students *below the surface* by investigating the role of language and culture within identity. Culture will take center stage as we integrate and honor learners' complex identities (and our own identities as well!). By acknowledging and leveraging the role of culture in language and in learning, we show our students and each other that our experiences and backgrounds matter. We can boost student outcomes by connecting to who students are and encouraging students to bring who they are into the classroom. We can view the classroom as a place of belonging that reflects all of our students, not as a rigid place where students of different backgrounds must fit in.

When we use our language lens, we think about our content and classroom culture from our students' perspectives to unpack how tricky academic language is and make it more explicit and accessible for students from various backgrounds. Realizing you are indeed a teacher of language no matter what content area(s) you teach is the first step to developing a language lens. Together we will unpack how our content areas have its own language and the *opportunities* that come with it. Not only does developing a language lens help us predict what challenges students may have, but it can also aid us in discovering opportunities to provide appropriate support and knowledge to plan explicit language goals. To make the target language more explicit, we need to understand more deeply what academic language is in our specific content areas, whether we teach biology, physical education, physics, kindergarten, guidance, college students, or in any other setting!

When you really think about the abundance of language and how important it is for teaching and learning, you may realize that a language lens will not only be useful for your MLL students but for your whole class in general.

All Teachers Are Language Teachers

If we speak English as our first language and live and work in an English-centric environment, we can easily take the English language for granted. When we are proficient in a language, we understand it, speak it, read it, and write it mostly without thinking, a process that can be as involuntary as breathing air. However, the language lens aims to make clear to all that the invisible nuances of language can be challenges for those new to it. For those who may be fully proficient and have never learned a new language, please know that nuances are very challenging. Learning a new language might even feel like remembering how and when to breathe! When we speak a language proficiently, we may not even notice how challenging it can be.

For example, why do we *park* in a *driveway* yet *drive* on a *parkway*? And how come *pineapples* consist of neither *pine* nor *apples*? Recall my earlier story of being a New Englander who moved to Wisconsin as a teenager; why do some parts of the United States refer to certain shoes as *sneakers* when we call them tennis shoes or even gym shoes in other places? English can be very confusing, and I'm not just talking about the technical, content-level vocabulary terminology. I'm talking about the way we *use* language, including figures of speech in connected text…and across different settings. Language is fluid. Language is cultural. Language is complex. As you'll discover in this guide, many aspects of language can be unnecessarily confusing for those learning it. What an opportunity! Our job as educators of students of any age is to analyze and predict those aspects to make them more visible to our students through engaging, rigorous, and language-rich classrooms.

At school, we have various academic settings where our students learn. In science class, we have academic science language. In math class, we have academic math language. In history class, we have academic history language. And yes, in English language arts (ELA), we do have a specific ELA language. If you're a teacher of health, physical education, technology, family / consumer education, art, or others, you have the language of your content area, too. Plus, no matter what we are teaching, we all use the general language of navigating the social and instructional experiences of school. In this way, we are all teaching language! Therefore, the challenge becomes ours as educators. How do we provide the appropriate support to differentiate our instruction for MLLs and ALLs so they can access deeper learning and perform at high levels? How do we ensure all of our students are included in learning spaces and set up for success at the Tier 1 , universal level? These are the questions at the heart of this book I ask you to answer for your unique school and your unique group of learners. But remember, as unique as our individual situations are, we are all charged with new ways of thinking about and teaching language as we teach in twenty-first-century classrooms! Plus, as coaches and leaders, your role is critical in imparting this message, along with key strategies, to all educators you support.

College-, Career-, Workplace- and Life-Readiness Standards

With the adoption of the more recent college and career-readiness standards, language moves into a more prominent role in every classroom, as it should! Every content area has its own language, just as every discipline or career field has its own acumen. How students use the target vocabulary and specific sentence structures and organize larger amounts of text into genres differs from, say, biology class to physical education class to literature class to theater class to algebra class. Understanding and using language effectively is what we want all learners to show us, that they know what we are teaching them, no matter what classroom we are in.

College- and career-readiness standards explicitly point out that academic language needs to be taught for students to better understand content and succeed in the workplace and life. Teaching language is no longer solely the role of the MLL teacher but of every content teacher in a school. Let me say that again: Teaching academic language so that students can actually understand and use it in content classrooms is no longer just the job of the language specialist. We all need to teach with a language lens. When we connect language and content to higher-order standards-based lessons, we intentionally make learning more meaningful and connected for all students.

Content teachers might think, *But I don't know how to teach language; I'm a chemistry teacher. Or I am a consumer education teacher. Or I am a 4th grade teacher. Or I teach engineering.* True, many teachers—in fact, vast amounts of the current workforce—simply were not trained to think about, never mind teach, the language of their content area. Unfortunately, that leaves many of us very underprepared to teach the students in front of us every day. Believe me, this is what I do in my daily work—I help schools and individual educators, including teachers, coaches, principals, directors, and support staff, bridge this gap. And sometimes, it feels like we can't bridge this gap fast enough with increasing student diversity and higher standards! We must remember that the gap is with *us,* as educators, needing to get up to speed on making our instruction accessible to ALL learners. The gap is not with the students!

A Sense of Urgency, Wrapped in Social-Emotional Support

The sense of urgency to improve our schools is immediate and challenging. Be it as it may, the new expectation is that all teachers implement language development techniques in their classes. Yet coaches and administrative leaders may struggle to understand how language and literacy must be integrated into classroom practice and professional development opportunities for all teaching staff. That's where *the language lens* comes in.

The key shifts of the college- and career-readiness standards include:

- A greater emphasis on literacy and language, including more focus on speaking and listening skills, as well as academic language in general, in all content classrooms
- A spiraling of complex text types across content areas from K–12
- A focus on text-based argumentative text or persuasive writing across grade levels

(Duguay, Massoud, Tabuka, Himmel, & Sugarman, 2013)

Those of us who have been promoting language and literacy across the curriculum know that these shifts are promising practices for all teachers K–12 and in any setting. Reading specialists and language specialists like me know that reading, writing, listening, and speaking academic language should be emphasized for all our students, particularly for those acquiring English and those not at grade level in literacy.

However, many teacher preparation programs, educator evaluation systems, and other institutional systems haven't previously focused on the nuances of language and culture. Language and culture should be the focus, not be an afterthought.

As I write this updated second edition of the book in 2023, I still see the same sense of urgency, coupled with the fallout from the coronavirus pandemic impacting our students at all ages like nothing we have seen in our lifetimes. The impact of the coronavirus pandemic is still being felt at all levels of our society, especially in our schools. Now is the time to improve our learning environments, which is likely why you're reading this book. I believe that we need to be less *reactive* and more *proactive*. Our students deserve that. Congratulations on reading this guidebook. This is one way of being proactive!

Part of being proactive is seeing social-emotional learning (SEL) as integral to academic learning. That means we focus on relationships and ensuring all students are ready to learn and their voices are heard. In classrooms, teachers can create a space for reflection on emotions, social interactions, and processes for making decisions. At the same time, at the school level, leaders can develop positive behavioral systems that are less punitive and more about being positive, mindful, and authentic (Honigsfeld, Dove, Cohan, McDermott Goldman, 2022). All in all, our schools should be places where students can learn how to learn as we model how to treat others within an equitable, democratic community.

Content Teachers and Language Specialists

Attending to language and how culture comes into play in classrooms is essential for not just MLLs but for ALLs—hence my focus on ALLs as well as MLLs in this book. Figure 1.1. shows how important the relationship is between content (in any classroom) and language (in any classroom). On one side, we have content, typically taught by the teacher, also known as the general education teacher, content teacher, or classroom teacher. This is where historically speaking, content is king, and teachers are trained to teach the content standards primarily. On the other side, we have language, often taught exclusively by language specialists, otherwise known as EL, ESL, MLL, ELD, ESOL, ENL, EAL teachers, or language specialists. Their role is primarily teaching English learners the language of content areas, very often in the form of language standards or specific language goals. As I mentioned earlier, however, it's important to remember that the work MLLs do with the language specialist, often called English Language Development (ELD), is *also* its own content area. Yet, all too often, ELD does not connect to the core content areas; in my experience, it should. That's what the language lens approach is all about. Connecting content to language and...language to content! The star in the middle of the Venn Diagram in Figure 1.1 is where this synergy can—and should—happen for students.

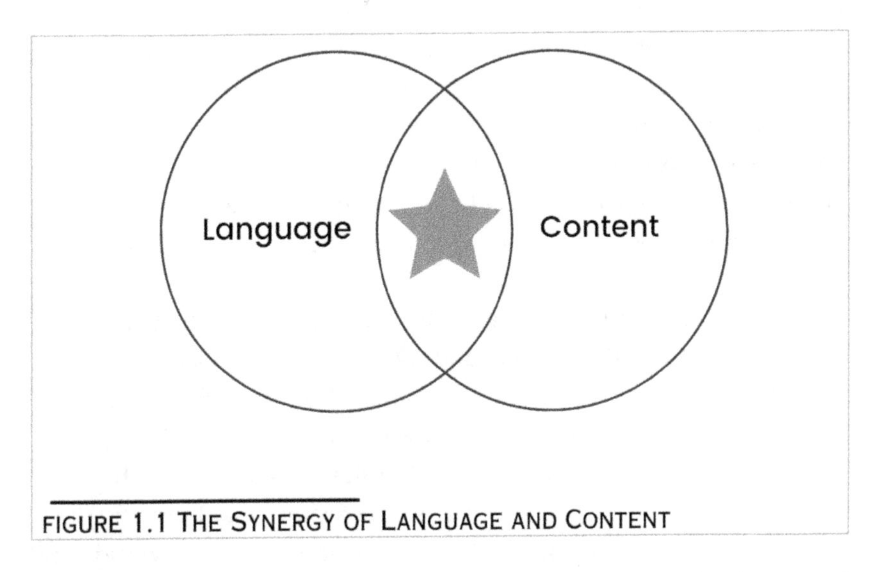

FIGURE 1.1 THE SYNERGY OF LANGUAGE AND CONTENT

How a language specialist supports MLLs can look several different ways depending on the local program model—it can look like separate services in an MLL classroom with just other MLL students all day; it can look like what has traditionally been called *pull-out* services, where the MLL teacher literally takes MLL students out of the general education classroom for some part of the school day for support. It can look like what has traditionally been called *push-in*, where the MLL teacher goes into the content classroom to work with the content teacher. It can look like actual co-teaching where the language specialist and the content teacher work as co-equals to plan, teach, and assess MLL and ALL students together, capitalizing on each other's strengths to bring a collaborative model to students. It can look like any combination thereof. This book is really geared towards the general education space, although many language specialists use it for validation of what they do with students in their own English Language Development space which can occur both inside and outside of the general education classroom.

Shifting Our Paradigm of School Culture

When we work with MLLs in schools, we are working with aspects of language, identity, and diversity within a cultural setting or institution, whether we realize it or not. Thus, in our roles as educators, we need to be aware of how minority languages and cultural groups have historically been perceived and treated in our schools. Then, we can see ourselves positioned in classrooms to either reinforce the historical paradigm or, as I encourage you to do, disrupt it as we strive towards a new, more inclusive paradigm. What is this new paradigm? And why do we need it?

The first part of this paradigm shift is an insistence that we break down the silos that separate and often stigmatize students from minority linguistic and cultural groups. The second part of this paradigm shift is redefining a *mainstream* classroom. The third part is to be self-aware individually and within the school system where we operate to intentionally center the learning around all of our students, not just one perspective, one culture, or one language. The world is in our classrooms.

Keep in mind that I have spent my teaching career as both a content specialist and as a language specialist in U.S. and international settings, so I've seen various schooling contexts—some that treat diversity as the asset it is and others that don't, devaluing the identities of students and families they are designed to serve. The devaluing may happen unintentionally, but the impact is what's important to measure. I support educators daily with the objective of providing more access to high-quality teaching and learning and anti-bias, anti-racist schooling that serves all of our students and families. This perspective I offer is the ideological foundation for why I wrote this book and why I do what I do every day as the founder and director of a professional learning organization focused on equity. We all need to approach our students through an equity-based mindset. We all need a toolkit to make our content come alive through language and literacy!

The Historical Paradigm

Back in the nineteenth century, schools in the U.S. were built on a factory model to meet the needs of the Industrial Revolution. Back then, the thought was that students needed standard skill sets for the workforce. However, now we are in the twenty-first century, a long way from the Industrial Revolution. Unfortunately, the mindset of standardized schooling hasn't always caught up with the need of time. Just think of how much things have changed since *you* were in school! Think about how much the model of schooling has not adequately adapted to keep up with our fast-paced, increasingly global society. We are constantly learning about technologies that make possible new ways of communicating and living. For example, map skills become almost obsolete in favor of learning how to navigate a smartphone app that guides us from point A to point B.

Although the rate of change can be boggling these days, the word *technology* is all relative. As the maxim goes about the invention of the car, "If we had asked people what they wanted, they would have said, *Faster horses.*" Indeed, horses were seen as technology, just like the first cars and steam locomotives. And now, we are looking at artificial intelligence as part of our daily life. Nothing, however, can replace the power of relationships and a language-rich learning environment. As we model at Confianza, let's bring a *high-tech, high-touch* approach to learning!

In our twenty-first-century schools, we need to keep in mind that many of the jobs we are preparing our students for likely don't all exist yet. The problems our students will be solving, and the industries they will be part of may be very different than the preparation our schools currently provide. Thus, we need to adapt the way we teach to catch up to the world outside of school. In schools, we need to move from *knowledge-telling* to *knowledge-building* and centralize the process of inquiry rather than simply following processes for some result (Hattie, 2023). We do not want any of our students to be left behind for reasons having to do with demographics or not having access to the power of language. Now, more than ever, we need to learn to listen and communicate with each other without defenses (Brown, 2017). Neither language nor cultural differences should stand in a child's way of realizing their potential and choosing their future dreams.

Some may forget that the history of innovation in the United States is laden with the success of those from other countries. In fact, many of the most accomplished entrepreneurs, inventors, athletes, and other innovators in the United States have been immigrants and first-generation immigrants (Florida, 2017; Global Citizen, 2018; Pofeldt, 2013; StarTalk, 2017), and the U.S. has more inventors from immigrant backgrounds than any other country combined (Kopf, 2017). What's more is that the percentage of immigrants in the U.S. is not only home to more immigrants than any other nation; over 13.6% of the population consists of immigrants, which is the same ratio it was about 100 years ago (Shoichet, 2023). While our MLL student population is not entirely comprised of immigrants, and all immigrants are not necessarily learning English as an additional language, it's essential to realize that migration is a common human condition we can all relate to.

Breaking Down the Silos

First, as part of this new paradigm shift, I'd like to see us as educators and as the field of education at large work toward more co-teaching instead of push-in, pull-out, or separate, silo-ed services only. Why is this important? Co-teaching, albeit challenging due to more intentional, coordinated collaboration between the language specialist and the general education teacher, can actually be more cohesive for all parties involved, most importantly, the students. The teachers—language specialist and general educator—can work toward the same goals, as opposed to two completely separate curricula, which are often disconnected from each other. When students have two different sets of goals and encounter different instructional languages from two teachers, it can be confusing and alienating. We want to make school more cohesive and inclusive for our MLL students, not what it has been historically—often disconnected and stigmatizing. Furthermore, we should be *modeling* for our students what collaboration looks, sounds, and feels like in all of its messiness and glory!

Certainly, some MLL students, as they move through their language development journey, require additional language-specific services, which may be done in a separate setting with a language specialist. This is not to say that separate language services shouldn't be done. Instead, I suggest considering the student's point of view when designing a set of instructional goals and a schedule so there is a through-line of what the student experiences and is expected to achieve regarding both language and content. You see, when teachers collaborate more intentionally, the language instruction and the content instruction can become more tied together, and we are actually setting students up for more success and more connection between language and content.

Redefining Mainstream

The second part of the new paradigm I offer is to rethink the concept of *general education*. The word *general*, when referring to classrooms, can also be interchanged with the word *regular* or, in my experience, more often than not, the word *mainstream*. Which term or terms have you heard to represent classrooms? What comes to your mind when you say general ed, regular ed, or *mainstream*? What exactly do we imply when we say *general, regular,* or *mainstream* education? In my work, I've heard all these words, which can imply that school is designed for students who meet the description of being from the dominant culture—which, historically speaking, has come to mean English-as-the-first-language, white, middle-class students who do not have disabilities. What I invite you to consider is that now in our diverse, global society, our demographics continue to diversify, the world is getting more and more connected, and, in turn, our school cultures are shifting. So, in response to these shifts, we need to change our classrooms. Schools need to operate less like twentieth-century models and more like ones that value and reflect our changing world.

Our Multifaceted Society and World

Have you ever heard the saying that schools are a microcosm of society? Well, if our society is reflected in our schools and our schools are more and more comprised of multilingual, multinational, multiracial, multiethnic, multicultural, multi-abled, multi-class populations, we should rethink the language that we use to describe our educational institutions, including our classrooms and our programs. Thus, I offer a new paradigm for what *general education* or *mainstream* classrooms can actually be. I challenge you to use the word *general,* not *mainstream* or *regular* (What is a *regular* student anyway?), until we come up with more innovative, accurate language as our institutions change to reflect our changing paradigm. Let's embrace the rich variety that our society brings to our classrooms and ensure that all teachers, not just language specialists, see themselves as educators who welcome, reach, teach, and celebrate diverse learners, all learners. Let's make sure that all students feel a sense of belonging so they can learn and chart their own course!

Mindset Matters

A major part of valuing the various cultural and linguistic assets of all students and families in our schools is not just getting to know them and integrating their identities in school but, most importantly, providing access and opportunities for them. As an educator told me, *We can't just say we value our MLLs. We must show it!* Yes, many times, actions speak louder than words. The mindset we have as educators really matters in shaping our actions. If we don't believe every child can reach high standards, our behaviors will reflect that in our classrooms. We want every student, including our language learners, to get access to our content through adequately supported, rigorous learning experiences.

We can change the historical paradigm, working toward more

collaboration and culturally and linguistically responsive instruction in every classroom by every teacher! More and more research and guidance are being focused in this area, often known as becoming more *linguistically responsive and sustaining.* We know now that classroom teachers need the following skills, all of which this guidebook explores with you:

- *Familiarity with students' linguistic and academic backgrounds.* Teachers need to listen to and get to know their students, to appreciate the distinct educational journeys, schooling histories, and unique needs of individual multilingual students.
- *An understanding of the language demands that go along with learning tasks.* This involves identifying vocabulary that students have to understand to access curriculum content; understanding the semantic and syntactic complexity of the language used in written instructional materials, and knowing the ways in which students are expected to use language to complete each learning task.
- *The skills to implement appropriate scaffolding,* so that MLLs can participate successfully in those learning tasks. Among the many scaffolding tools and strategies teachers can use:

1. Extra-linguistic supports (visual tools like pictures, maps, or videos, or data visualizations like graphs and timelines; illustrations, maps, and videos)
2. Supplementing or amplifying challenging texts to make them more accessible (creating study guides, for example)
3. Supplementing or amplifying the oral language used in your classroom to reduce the burden on MLLs (for instance, by minimizing idiomatic expressions, pausing more often, or giving students lesson outlines)
4. Giving clear, explicit instructions
5. Encouraging students' use of home languages
6. Creating purposeful activities so that MLLs have opportunities to interact with others and negotiate meaning

7. Minimizing the anxiety that MLLs might feel in a classroom of native English speakers; setting norms and rules that prevent teasing

(Lucas, Villegas, and Freedson, 2008 as cited in Usable Knowledge)

If we focus on what is in common between language teachers and content teachers, we find rich opportunities to focus on not just MLLs but also ALLs. Additionally, we find collaboration opportunities so teachers can learn from one another for the benefit of more culturally and linguistically responsive and sustaining instruction, no matter what age or content they teach. We can envision and create a new paradigm where everyone benefits.

Standards-Based Instruction

To start our language lens journey with the end in mind, let's imagine what we want for all our students. I think we can agree that we all want every student, regardless of demographic, to reach the goal of learning at high levels so that they can explore their interests and reach their potential in life. To have students achieve at high levels, we need to have clear standards for them to reach with our support. This book will not teach or review with you the specific content standards for your content area. What this book will do, however, is show you how to take your content standards and teach them with a language lens so that all language learners have an opportunity to access the content you are teaching. If we start with this end in mind, we can envision all of our students learning grade-level standards at high levels of cognitive rigor.

As we will explore in our journey, the goal is not to lower the standards but rather design instruction for all, honoring all backgrounds that enter our schools. We do not want language learners to be excluded from access to grade-level standards and deeper learning. We want to keep standards high and tasks complex yet scaffold the way students access this learning, not water it down. If you are familiar with *universal design*, you will appreciate this approach. An example of universal design is when a building is designed so that all people, whether they are able-bodied or are using a wheelchair or walker, can enter a building together using a sloped entrance that includes everyone at the same level.

FIGURE 1.2 GRADE LEVEL STANDARDS = THE MOUNTAIN

Let's use a mountain as a metaphor for high standards for all (See Figure 1.2.). If the learning target, or set of content standards, for any given unit and the sequential lessons that comprise that unit can be compared to the top of a mountain, we want all students to get there. However, we know that not every student is the same. Students can come from very different backgrounds, including different cultural and linguistic groups. Students come to us with varying experiences in the community and in the world at large, beyond our brick-and-mortar schools. There is no one-size-fits-all for how we can teach learners and no one pathway up the mountain. Some students may need a bit more time. Some may need navigation tools. Some students may need the route explained to them in several different ways, while others may need to work with another student or group of students to make meaning of this journey. If we think about being responsive to our students' needs as creating differentiation pathways for them as they all go up the proverbial mountain, then we begin to create a classroom that includes all students so they can be successful.

Accommodations vs. Modifications

In our journey through the language lens approach, I find it helpful to remind educators of the difference between *accommodations* and *modifications*. Accommodations remove barriers to learning in the general education classroom so that all students have access where modifications are changes to what is taught (Reading Rockets, 2020). The example above about guiding students up the mountain exemplifies accommodations. That's really what this guide is about. We are not having multilingual learners climb different mountains. That would be modifying the learning standard. Students should all be climbing the same mountain, albeit through different routes and perhaps with different tools. We are not modifying the content so that students learning English are working towards different grade level standards. That would be *watering down* the rigor of the grade level curriculum.

I find myself respectfully asking educators to watch their language in this regard. For example, I hear, *We need to modify what this MLL is being taught since they are just learning English.* I then respond, *It sounds like you're trying to provide access to the grade level standard, not change the standard itself, right? Remember: the language lens is about* accommodating *or* amplifying *language, not modifying the standard. Let's try using the term* accommodate *or* amplify *instead.* As you can see, it's a small but important change in language.

High Expectations for ALL Students

We want all students to have access to perform at high standards in the service of an equitable, democratic education, no matter what or where we teach. That is the purpose of public education, and if you're in a private school, it is likely part of your mission there, too. When we teach language learners, it's important to keep in mind that although we can understand the scope and sequence of skills and concepts, we want to avoid *watering down* or *modifying* the content, which results in students not being taught grade-level content standards. Sadly, this is part of the history of the MLL population—lowering standards, rescuing, or remediating instead of scaffolding to high standards with differentiation pathways for students to access content. We need to reverse this trend and make sure the onus is on us because every educator is in a position to positively influence how their students learn. It's an exciting opportunity when you think about it! Let's raise the bar, figuratively speaking.

Very often, teachers come to me frustrated because, while they know their standards need to be at grade level for their MLLs, they don't know how to support or scaffold the academic language required to reach those standards. The impulse may be to lower the bar versus keep the bar at grade level while *amplifying the language of what is being taught.* That's what we are going to tackle in this book—the how: the practices for ensuring your classroom is language-rich with meaningful learning experiences for your culturally and linguistically diverse students and all your students. Additionally, an ongoing self-examination of our belief systems about all students being capable of and entitled to perform at high standards is an important layer of this work. A synthesis of research reviewed by Nora and Echevarria (2016) shows that when teachers have low expectations of students, often students of color and from less advantaged backgrounds, teacher actions reflect those lowered expectations by behaviors such as giving less challenging assignments to those students and calling on them less often. Low expectations can create a self-fulfilling prophecy. As stated earlier, mindset matters!

We need to hold all students, including MLLs, to these high standards. This requires us as educators to more deeply understand content standards and their progressions through the grades. For example, when I was a fourth-grade teacher, I would try to get to know the standards vertically, third grade through fifth grade. That way, I could be prepared to understand what students should know to reach my grade-level content, *scaffolding down*. Plus, I would also be more able to know where they were going so I could extend their learning when it was appropriate, *scaffolding up*. Understanding curricular scope and sequence in this way allows us to see the learning trajectory of skills and concepts in our content area so that we may more appropriately tier instruction vertically to meet learners' needs.

Focusing on common academic language across the entire school day is an incredible way to support students' transfer skills as they go up the mountain. If educators make the *language functions* more visible and supported, students can connect across content areas and into life outside of school, too. Language functions are also typically tier 2 vocabulary terms which we will discuss in Chapter 3. For example, when we reveal the language of *cause and effect,* students learn the function of causality. In science class, we learn that if we don't water a plant, the plant will die. In literature class, we learn about a character who persisted and was then able to accomplish their goal. In math class, we learn about compounded interest due to not paying off debt. In life outside school, we see that when it rains, the barbecue may be canceled. Cause and effect language includes the terms *cause and effect,* but it can also include less visible signal terms like: *after, although, as, when, while, until, because, before, if, since, as a result of, consequently, due to, lead to, resulted in.* We can ask questions like, *What happened? What happened as a result of…?"* and answer questions with stems like, *"Due to the fact that…" or "The reason most likely for…was…."* We can also illustrate cause and effect with a simple yet powerful graphic organizer, like Figure 1.3 shows. The clues to decode the function of language are everywhere, and we can equip our students with the tools to be successful in many contexts.

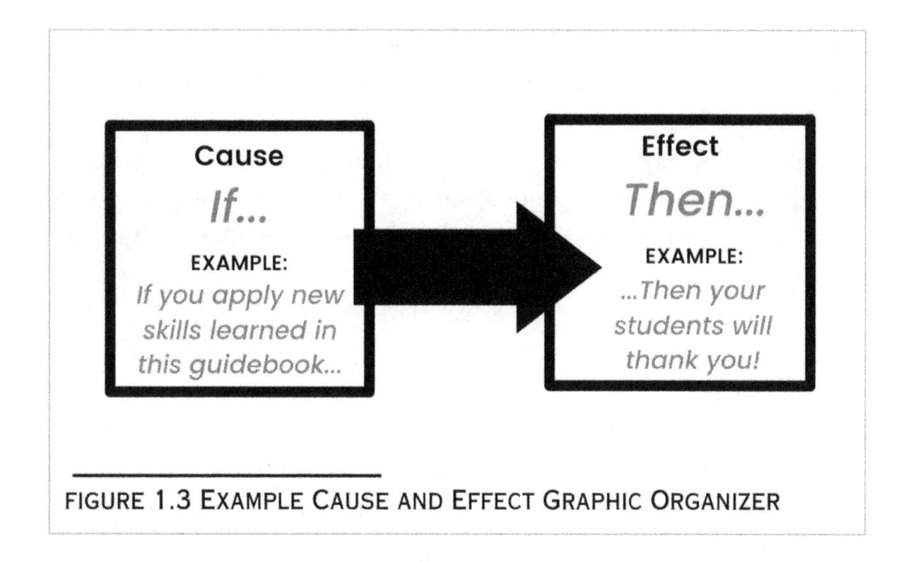

FIGURE 1.3 EXAMPLE CAUSE AND EFFECT GRAPHIC ORGANIZER

How This Book Is Organized

This chapter has presented an introduction for you on the language lens. At the end of this chapter, you will find a self-assessment that I encourage you to take before continuing to Chapter 2. The self-assessment will help you focus the reading and application of new practices on your needs. You may even use the results to shape your Action Cycle®, should you choose to use that tool for personalized inquiry. When you take the self-assessment, you may discover that you are more effective in some of these practices and less effective in others, and that's okay! If you are a coach or leader, please take the self-assessment thinking about the educator or educator you are supporting, or, better yet, take it together to build a shared vision! Overall, my hope is that through this simple self-assessment reflection process, you and/or your team can focus on an area of focus within your sphere of influence that you can immediately learn about and apply in your classroom for the benefit of your students. Instructional leaders will be asked throughout this guide to *systematize* improvements so that the whole school (or district) benefits!

In Chapter 2, we will discover how we can get to know our students and integrate what they bring into our classroom environment. In Chapter 3, we will analyze aspects of academic language to successfully plan our language goals. In Chapter 4, we will drill down into effective language and literacy strategies that can work for engaging students in what we call the four domains of language—reading, writing, listening, and speaking. In Chapter 5, we will learn about appropriate supports to differentiate our instruction so students can access high content standards.

The Competencies

These chapters each represent a *competency area* that supports language learners in content classrooms, or what I will refer to as *The Language Lens Competencies for Teachers, Leaders, and Coaches*. The competencies are introduced in this guidebook, and they can all be explored further, yet this guidebook is an overview, a starting point for the competencies. The first chunk of each chapter is for all educators to review, whether you are a teacher, coach, or leader. At the end of each chapter, I will share some implementation ideas for two distinct groups: 1) for teachers, including potential next steps for self-study or teaming with your department or grade level, plus ways to leverage the expertise of your language specialist, and 2) for coaches and leaders to support educators you work with in these practices, whether that support be individual with educators, in teams or both. As previously mentioned, this book is for educators who work with students of all ages, so please adapt the practices as needed for your students' developmental levels. Moreover, as I mentioned earlier, language specialists may find the entire guide useful for validating what you currently do and even find some talking points for collaborating with leadership and your colleagues.

CHAPTER 1 (THIS CHAPTER) BEGINS OUR JOURNEY WITH A LANGUAGE LENS:

- Essential Question for ALL Educators, Especially Teachers: How Do We Start Developing our Language Lens?

- Essential Question for Coaches/Leaders: How Can We Ensure High Expectations that Positively Impact Our Professional Learning Culture?

Chapter 2 is all about culture and identity:

- Essential Question ALL Educators, Especially Teachers: How Do We Center Those Students in Our Classrooms Who May Be on the Margins?
- Essential Question for Leaders/Coaches: How Can All Learners' Identities be Affirmed as Part of an Equitable Learning Culture?

Chapter 3 focuses on the power of language goals:

- Essential Question for ALL Educators, Especially Teachers: How Do We Infuse Language within Our Content Objectives/Goals?
- Essential Question Coaches/Leaders: How Can Clear Goals Drive Change at the Classroom Level and School Level?

Chapter 4 gets into language and literacy practices for any classroom:

- Essential Question for ALL Educators, Especially Teachers: How Do We Ensure Language-Rich Learning Spaces for All Learners?
- Essential Question for Coaches/Leaders: How Do We Support Educators in their Development of Inclusive, Engaging, Language-Rich Classrooms?

. . .

CHAPTER 5 DISCUSSES SCAFFOLDS FOR INPUT AND OUTPUT:

- Essential Questions for ALL Educators, Especially Teachers: How Will You Add to Your Toolbox So That You Can Implement Language Routines and Scaffolds?
- Essential Questions for Coaches/Leaders: How Do We Sustain and Scale Systemic Practices for Maximum Impact Across Our School?

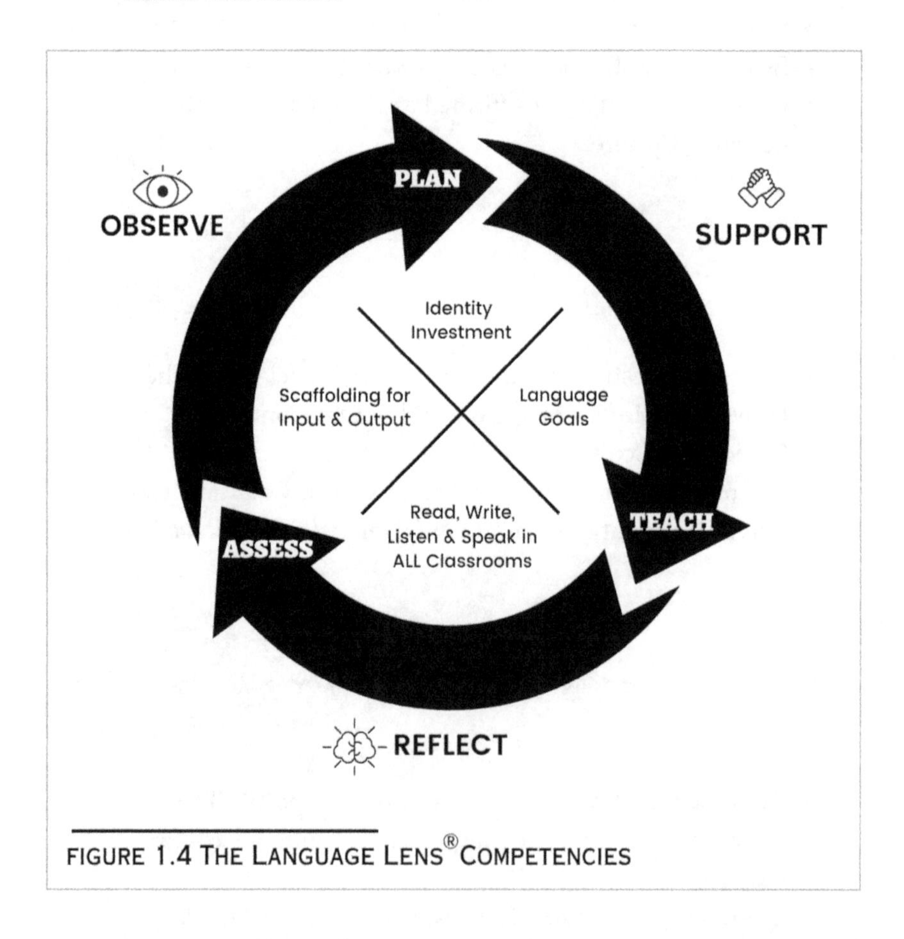

FIGURE 1.4 THE LANGUAGE LENS® COMPETENCIES

In Figure 1.4, you see the overview of these competencies in a cycle, *The Language Lens Competencies for Teachers, Leaders, and Coaches.* You can also find a downloadable overview of the competencies with the essential questions for each at languagelens.com. Consider how the competences discussed in each chapter are inside the cycle. Then, consider how the actions of *observe, support,* and *reflect* are situated around the cycle. Why? As we've already touched on earlier in this chapter, reflecting is essential to being an educator, no matter how long you've been at it! We are truly never done learning. I find that making sacred time to reflect on what's going well, what needs to be improved, and what resources I could benefit from in my practice as an educator (now as an educator of educators, to be specific!) is what drives my growth and, more importantly, my impact on schools. I've been at this a long time, and I have so much yet to learn. Reflection helps me see my progress, what blind spots I may not be seeing, and what areas of growth to work on in my practice. It's the same for any educator, and I hope you agree. We all have our own lived experiences and our own blind spots. As John Dewey, a key player in the history of education in the United States, reminds us, "We do not learn from experience, we learn from reflecting on experience."

Additionally, the habits of observing and supporting should be part of any coach and leader's daily schedule. I've included tips for coaches and leaders as they observe, support and reflect with teachers. However, classroom teachers can observe and support each other, too. As I'll guide you in the end-of-chapter pointers, many opportunities exist for peer observation and support. Just like with our students, we want to build independence as teachers and as learners. Educators are learners, too. I believe learners of all ages and levels should participate in what I call *parallel practices*. We need to model what we want for students for learners of all ages. So anything you read in this guide is also what I model when I'm teaching adults!

Reflecting on your Current Practice

You'll see in the following self-assessment that you can reflect on the language lens competencies to see what areas you could improve upon as you read this guide. Teachers, take the assessment thinking about your own practice. Coaches/Leaders, take the assessment on behalf of those you support or with those you support, whether it be one educator, one team, one grade level, one department, or your entire staff.

Use your self-assessment results to guide your professional learning as you read this guidebook. You may want to read through the guide end to end, or you may want to zero in on what matters to you in your practice. I've written this guide using the same kind of approachable tone and language I use in the courses and workshops I teach and the coaching I provide. I hope you find this book to be useful. I'm a guide at your side, even if I can't be with you in person!

The Language Lens Self-Assessment

If you are a coach or leader, answer each question thinking holistically about the skills of the educators you support or an individual educator or team you support. I invite you to also take this self-assessment *with* colleagues or *with* those you coach or supervise. You can also download a one-pager version of this self-assessment at languagelens.com. Use the following scale to self-assess your current practices:

1 = Never heard of this before
2 = Heard of this but don't know it
3 = Know it but can't explain it
4 = Know and and can explain it
5 = Know it and can teach it to someone else

1. I get to know my students' backgrounds, including their English language proficiency levels (if they are multilingual), literacy levels, academic histories, schooling experiences, and home and cultural factors. (Chapter 2)
2. I plan practical, student-friendly language goals for my units of study. (Chapter 3)
3. I ensure that every lesson I teach has students not just listening but purposefully speaking, reading, and writing, too. (Chapter 4)

4. I provide various scaffolds for students to reach content standards, including various strategies for student ownership/agency. (Chapter 5)
5. I know how to utilize the human resource that is my language specialist (if applicable). (All chapters)
6. I work with my team to collaborate around not just curriculum planning but students' needs. (All chapters)

Confianza's Action Cycle® as a Tool for Immediate Inquiry

As a companion to this guidebook, I'm excited to share with you a central process we use at Confianza to make the inquiry process tangible and accessible to all educators. When you visit our resource site at languagelens.com, you'll see resources about Action Cycle® for Implementing Equity, Language, and Literacy Practices in Schools in the professional learning category. I invite you to refer to this resource for added structure in your professional learning experience here through this guidebook. At Confianza, each participant of our online courses completes an Action Cycle to show how they will or did implement new learning into their practice *right away*! We have a constantly growing collection of these educator-driven cycles that show change right away for students and their educators. The Action Cycle® is essentially a mini-action research project. Yet any day of the week, you, dear reader, can easily conduct your own mini-cycle of inquiry that is ongoing, iterative, and based on trying out new practices that your students need now.

Educational leader Damaris Gutierrez explains that when we try out new skills in our classrooms, "[The Action Cycle®] *is a great way to really involve teachers in their own professional development because they are invested in it. They get to decide the work they want to do but still having that accountability piece embedded in their reflection…What could I do differently, and how could I move forward with it? We're not expecting it to be perfect the first time around*" (Confianza, 2018). The idea is to focus on what is within your sphere of influence in your classroom (if you are a teacher) or your team/department/school (if you are a coach or leader). We can build more efficacy when we drive our professional learning and see the results as soon as possible! Figure 1.5 shows the steps of the Action Cycle®, and the guiding questions are listed below to support your ongoing inquiry. Find the complete process at languagelens.com.

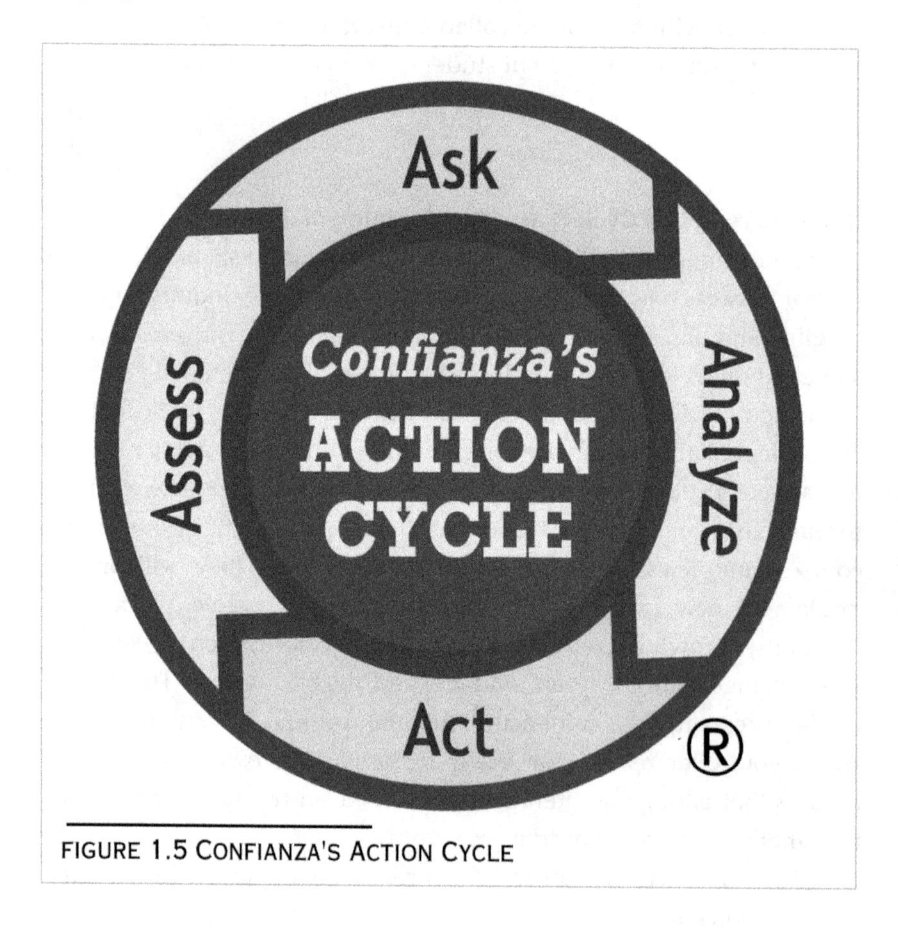

FIGURE 1.5 CONFIANZA'S ACTION CYCLE

ASK: What is the key issue you're facing around supporting your students (MLL and/or ALL) within your sphere of influence? What would success look like if you addressed this issue?

ANALYZE: What data shows that this is an issue to focus on? What are your current successes? What are your current challenges or opportunities to improve?

ACT: What specific steps can you take? What is the timeline and the benchmarks? What resources do you need?

ASSESS (later on, after you implemented your Action Plan): What happened? What data can we look at? What was the student impact? What else can we do to improve?

TIPS FOR TEACHERS: HOW DO WE GET STARTED WITH DEVELOPING OUR LANGUAGE LENS?

1. What are your professional and/or student learning objectives for this school year? How can this book guide you to focus on one or two of those goals? Can you choose one or more of the competencies described earlier in the self-assessment to go deep on and connect to goals you are already working on?

2. Take stock of your collaboration resources for content and your collaboration resources for language. Who is on your grade-level or department team with whom you can collaborate? Does your school or district have a language specialist or a team of language specialists with whom you can consult and collaborate? Do you know what the role of the language specialist is in your school/district? When do you meet with these colleagues? When could you meet? Have you discussed who your language learners are? Have you worked with any of the above educators to focus on student needs, especially in terms of language needs? Is your team receptive to trying out new practices together? If so, how can you deepen this collaboration to serve your language learners? If not, how can you begin?

• • •

3. Are there ways you can collaborate with your content team members, your language specialist, and/or a coach to help you implement what you learn in this guide? Here are some ideas to do on your own or with a team:

4. Be clear about your roles. Ask the language specialist what his or her role is for both working with students and, if applicable, working with teachers. Find times to meet consistently, and try to stick to that schedule, even if it only means collaborating virtually instead of face-to-face.

5. Establish norms for collaboration. For example, *We will meet at our agreed-upon times and bring our expertise to the table, focusing on student needs.* Realize that collaboration relationships take time and effort. Plus, honesty is important as we come together from different perspectives to serve our shared students. Revisiting norms is just as important as creating them, so make time to come together, reflect, and revise norms as needed. See the articles about collaboration at langaugelens.com for more information.

6. Keep students at the center yet learn from one another. Co-create goals for MLLs that both of you can work on. Let the language specialist know what is coming up in the curriculum and provide background information and key concepts to help build his or her capacity in your content area. Also, don't hesitate to consult with your language specialist to learn more about bringing the language lens into your classroom for MLLs and ALLs!

7. Discuss the ways you can collaborate for the benefit of the students. If the MLLs do not need separate language instruction, think of ways to create more collaborative instructional models. It's not enough for language instruction to only occur within this language development time with a specialist; content teachers can and should practice ways

for MLLs and ALL students to engage in their content area through language and literacy as well.

8. Remember to refer to your local programmatic guidelines for this since there are typically state, district, and school regulations, policies, and guidance on local instructional models. If you have the freedom to be creative about how you approach instructing your shared students, consider how co-teaching could work. Co-planning is a great thing to make co-teaching work, but if you don't have that, invite the specialists to be part of your lessons and add their thoughts and ideas as you teach. Confer with your leadership on how more structured collaboration time can be planned for the benefit of students. As the saying goes, two heads can be better than one!

TIPS FOR COACHES AND LEADERS: HOW CAN WE ENSURE HIGH EXPECTATIONS THAT POSITIVELY IMPACT OUR PROFESSIONAL LEARNING CULTURE?

1. Remember how I said professional learning is a culture, not a single event. How would you describe the professional learning culture of your school? Is it reflective and healthy? Is it psychologically safe for all staff to take risks within a culture of learning? What's working? What's not working so far? If you need more specific tips on fostering psychologically safe spaces for your staff, check out the leading for equity resources at languagelens.com.

2. Can you name the professional learning spaces that educators have access to? Is there sacred, structured time built into the schedule for collaboration? For example, Professional Learning Communities (PLCs)? Common Planning Time (CPT)? What structural barriers in the schedule must be broken down and updated to foster more focused collaboration and teaming across the school? Are educators supported

in these spaces? Is the language specialist given a platform to share expertise and student supports? If so, how? If not, how could you more effectively support and guide educators to have true collaboration focused on student outcomes?

3. As I explained in this chapter, a leader's greatest power is to shape the narrative of the school culture. In your school, do you have a shared vision of equitable instruction for Tier 1/universal instruction? Can you list simple look-fors you expect in every classroom? How do you/your team communicate this vision? Is everyone moving in the same direction towards this vision? Do all educators know that they need to share responsibility for all students? What common practices and protocols need to be implemented to ensure this time is maximized to focus on students? Are the professional learning spaces (e.g., PLCs, CPTs) functioning? Are expectations clear? What could be improved? If you need a refresher, see the articles at languagelens.com in the professional learning category.

4. Please keep in mind that language is powerful, and, as leaders, people are listening to our words and watching our actions. For example, what language do you model appropriate for serving all students? For example, do staff use terms like, your students or my students to describe different subgroups? Could those silos be broken down so that everyone collectively uses the term *our kids*? Could different terms be used to build shared responsibility and a shared knowledge base among staff to support all students? See the resources for leading for equity at languagelens.com for more tips on building shared responsibility and shared language.

5. Do you have a language specialist or a team of language specialists? Is their role clear or is it ambiguous? Are they overburdened? Are they underutilized? Do they understand what is within their sphere of influence as a critical resource? How can you support this key change

agent? How can you communicate their role to the entire staff? At languagelens.com, check out the professional learning resources, where you'll find the article, *Our Kids: The Role of the Language Specialist*. You can read it with your language specialists and use the text together as a jumping point for proactive change.

6. I spend much of my daily work reminding coaches and leaders to go back to basics and make sure we are building respectful, choice-based professional learning that is relevant and meaningful for educators, for adult learners, as it were. As an instructional leader, do you refer to adult learning theory to guide your professional learning planning and implementation? If you need a refresher, go to languagelens.com for resources on supporting adult learning in the professional learning category.

7. If you evaluate educators, do you evaluate accurately? In other words, do you reward less-than-proficient instructors with proficient scoring? If so, how could you recalibrate expectations to be high and student-centered? Furthermore, when you hire, could you recruit educators and any staff across your school with positive and impactful experiences with multilingual learners? Add these important criteria to your list when interviewing, hiring, and placing staff.

8. Going back to a clear vision of equitable instruction for all students, do you have clear look-fors—what you expect equitable instruction to be--across all spaces in your school? Are these look-fors easy to recall and explain to teachers and families? Consider creating a clear set of look-fors with your leadership team, calibrate on what they look, sound, and feel like. Share these look-fors with staff and families to create a shared understanding of what we want for all students. Check out the examples of schoolwide change for leaders at languagelens.com

• • •

9. What lessons did you, your team, and/or your school community learn from the pandemic? Have you reflected on that trauma and collective learning with your team, and your staff? If so, what did you learn, and how are you bringing those lessons into your leadership? If not, could you back up to reflect and ask community members what lessons were learned in order to improve the school?

CHAPTER 2
IDENTITY INVESTMENT

THIS CHAPTER FOCUSES ON THE LANGUAGE LENS COMPETENCY OF STUDENT identity investment: getting to know our students for culturally and linguistically responsive and sustaining teaching and learning.

- ESSENTIAL QUESTION FOR ALL EDUCATORS: How Do We Center Those Students in Our Classrooms Who May Be on the Margins?
- ESSENTIAL QUESTION FOR COACHES AND LEADERS: How Can All Learners' Identities be Affirmed as Part of an Equitable Learning Culture?

Educators must learn about integrating student identities to ensure they have a safe, respective, and engaging learning environment in which to learn and develop autonomy (Moll, 1992; Cummins et al., 2005; González, Moll, & Amanti, 2005; Little, Dam & Legenhausen, 2017; Sharma, & Christ, 2017). This critical part of the language lens approach means that educators must learn about students' strengths, interests, and cultural and linguistic backgrounds and strive to incorporate these aspects into our classrooms. Identity investment is a precursor to active and meaningful learning.

. . .

But First...Getting to Know Ourselves

Before we even start thinking about how to get to know our students, we need to ask ourselves, *Who am I? What is my story? How do I identify myself? How do aspects of my identity impact my practice as an educator?* Even though we may never fully understand what it's like to walk in someone else's shoes, we can stand in solidarity with our students, affirming and integrating their identities in our classrooms and our school community. Yet it may be hard to see what our students need from us until we first do some self-examination. Let me model this process for you, starting with my own identity.

When I look inward at how I identify myself as an educator, I first think of my *why*. Why am I an educator? What is my mission statement? *I am an educator because I believe that all students should have opportunities to learn and live to their potential. I help identify and remove barriers to these opportunities as a leader and agent of positive change.* You may want to take a few minutes to stop and jot. Why are you an educator? What is your mission statement?

Then, to go deeper into why I am an educator and what has shaped my identity as an educator, I think back to what has brought me here today and what has shaped me. Here I share with your five stories from my journey that have helped shape my identity:

1. Throughout my entire school career, I wore hand-me-down clothes. In elementary school, I was labeled as *a free and reduced lunch kid*. In middle school, I was teased by the wealthier girls and felt like a *have not* in a *have/have not* community. I tried to overcompensate for this perceived lack by overachieving as a scholar, getting labeled as *gifted and talented*, and winning writing and poetry recitation contests. However, underneath, I was ashamed of my status. For example, in elementary school, I did everything I could to hide the fact that I wasn't giving the lunch lady any money in the lunch line. In fact, I pretended to give her coins while she graciously winked at me, opening her hand for money that was not there. I have unconsciously developed a winking habit when interacting with students who seem to

be uncomfortable or nervous because of how the kindness of the lunch lady made me feel safe.

2. I am the oldest of four siblings, and my youngest sister was born with a rare, non-congenital birth defect and multiple physical and learning disabilities. For much of my childhood, my sister was hospitalized for dozens of surgeries, starting with the NICU. Upon her birth in my fourth grade, I instantly became a helper and teacher, caring for my other siblings alongside my aunts while my parents were at the hospital. I took sign language classes with my parents and then taught these signs to my siblings so we could communicate with our sister during her hearing-impaired years. I witnessed multiple life-or-death medical events. I encountered ruthless bullying of my sister that I learned to stand up to on her behalf. I watched my parents advocate incessantly for my sister's IEP to be implemented correctly. I am aware that as an able-bodied person, I have certain access and opportunities that my sister with disabilities inherently doesn't. I attribute being an educator, an ally, and an advocate for others whose voices are not always heard directly to being a sibling to my youngest sister.
3. After freshman year of high school, my family moved to a different part of the United States with a very different regional culture and somewhat different lexicon. Where I grew up on Cape Cod, I had about fifty students in my class and then, when I was transplanted to a suburban area near Madison, Wisconsin, I had almost three-hundred students in my class. I had to start completely over; making friends, navigating a huge high school, and eating lunch by myself. Because of this experience, I can connect to our newcomer and immigrant students and any new school student, especially if they are from an entirely different place.
4. In my junior year of high school, I got labeled an *at risk* student. In my sophomore year, I was sexually assaulted and did not know how to report it or advocate for myself. This

trauma added to the compounded trauma I had already experienced in my life. I hid away and felt totally disconnected from the overachieving Sarah I was back in elementary and middle school. I skipped school and eventually ran away from home. The assistant principal at my high school is the one who helped pull me from the darkness, letting me know that I was seen by him. He told me that he wanted me to graduate high school and that I could if I focused on it. He even got me a "job" in the high school office during my study hall so I wouldn't be tempted to keep skipping. Because of this part of my identity, I fiercely stand for trauma-informed practices, integrated social-emotional learning, and policies that protect all groups, especially our most vulnerable students.

5. When I made it to college, I did not take college seriously because it was too easy, and I didn't see the relevancy in my required courses. I slipped back to my invisible, unresolved trauma, which spiraled into full-blown clinical depression. In order to stabilize, I had to leave my university far from home, and live with my parents to get mental health treatment. After five years and three university campuses, I became the first person in my family to graduate with a college degree. From there, I found my passion for teaching so that others don't miss opportunities like I almost did. This experience taught me not to stigmatize mental health or take education for granted. I believe it's our role as educators to help students find their own path and passion.

When people learn about these parts of who I am, I was not always a high achieving learner but a struggling, at risk student who was bullied, who defended her sister from bullies and who has been extremely unstable and uncertain at times, they are often surprised. As they say, there's more than meets the eye because so much of who we are exists *below the surface.* So much of who we are as people, so much of our identities, are not what we see but what we don't see. That's why we don't want to make assumptions about each other or jump to conclusions. This leads to *stereotyping*. Who I am and what has shaped my identity are largely not visible. For example, while I was born into a household with English as our primary language, between my siblings and our partners, our family now constitutes a total of four languages other than English. If you count my extended family, there's more; my father-in-law speaks five languages, and I hear his accent as a window into his multilingual brain. While I was born in the U.S., I have chosen to live and work in different countries, and I have taught students from over 40 linguistic groups. I try to continuously learn many different greetings in other languages and model this in the professional learning I lead as a voluntary language learner.

A more visible aspect of my identity is that I am a white woman who started her teaching career teaching mostly students of color. I knew that my background was very different from those I was teaching. I quickly realized that I had blind spots, and biases, and I still do. As a white woman, I represent the vast majority of educators in the United States (Will, 2020), which is a problem, by the way, since we need educators to reflect all groups. Nevertheless, as a white woman, I have a platform that I take very seriously, striving to stand for others who do not have this same kind of platform.

Everyone should have a platform and opportunities, yet we don't live in an equitable society. As an auntie of biracial children, I am even more accurately aware of the risks my niece and nephew may encounter in school and in the larger society simply because of the color of their skin. I also am an auntie to two Jewish children who are part of a religious group that is, unfortunately, also targeted for their identity. While I will never understand what racism and antisemitism feel like, I can try to be an ally and stand up for what's right by standing in solidarity with those who face injustices every day. Because of my experiences that have profoundly shaped my identity as an educator, I stand beside my students, clients, and groups as an ally, not a white savior. I must continuously grow, learn and be humble. To me, it's not about politics; it's about being human and making sure all humans belong so they can learn to their potential.

All of these experiences and more make me who I am. I can organize the big aspects of my identity I shared with you here in an *identity map* (see Figure 2.1). These experiences and aspects of my identities—seen and unseen—inform *my about the 'why'* of being an educator. I must constantly put myself in the position of listener, learner, and ally. Our identities are complex, and multi-faceted, and they impact how we see others. Our identities shape our biases, behavior, language and actions about others. I must constantly check and recheck myself. Now I ask you, how can you unpack aspects of your own identity for yourself? How does your identity inform how you educate students? How does your identity inform your *'why'* of being an educator? How can you show that identity as a social agent? How does your story impact your work? We all have stories that make us who we are.

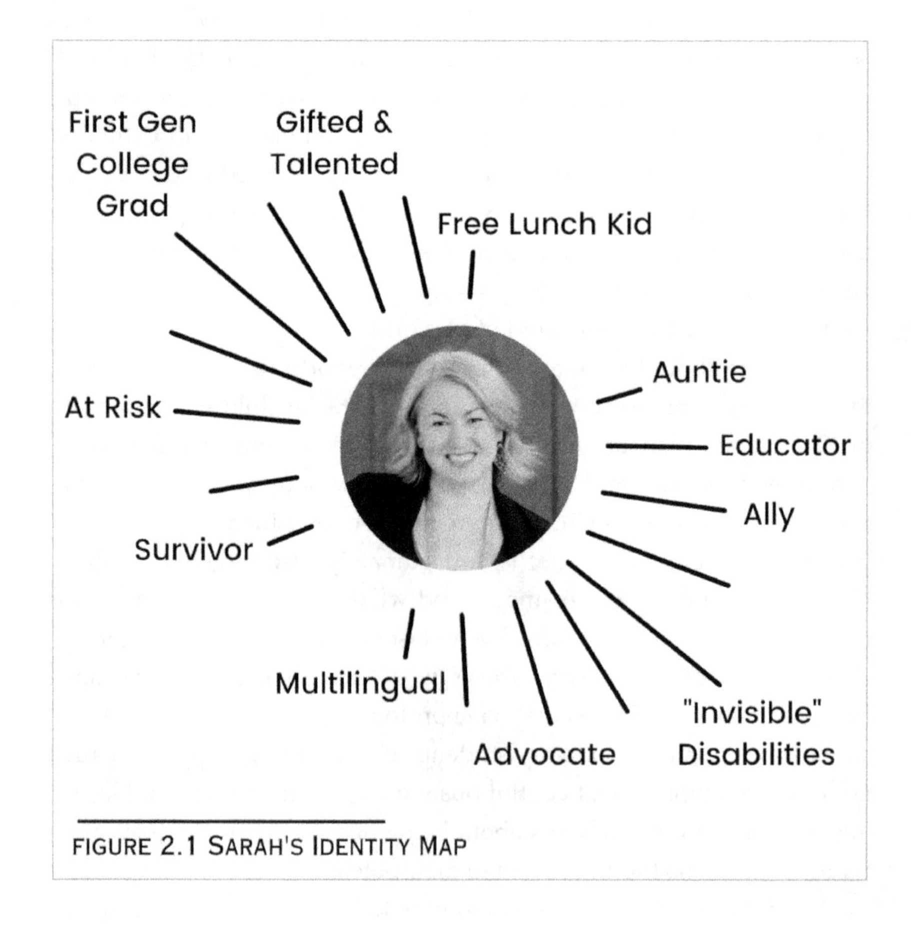

FIGURE 2.1 SARAH'S IDENTITY MAP

Getting to Know Our Students

One of my favorite sayings I kept in mind as a teacher and now as a consultant is: *Kids don't care what you know until they know that you care*—that is, we can have the most well-planned and thought-out lessons and tips and strategies and standards with which to teach, but if we don't connect with our students, we won't get very far. As another saying goes, *It's all about relationships.*

We need to make sure we understand what students are bringing to school to connect with them well and help them engage in our content area. This is the foundation for all strong teaching that differentiates by not just academic needs but linguistic needs and social-emotional needs. Infusing technology mindfully is critical as well, especially in this (semi) post-COVID era. Multilingual educator and writer Sarah Said (2023) believes we need to explain to students the importance of being present as part of our integrated social-emotional learning approach. For example, in her classroom, at the start of each class, Mrs. Said sets the scene in her secondary classroom for all students to get ready to learn. First, each student uses their phone to check in with her, their teacher, privately. Then, students complete an assignment; some call these Bell Ringers or Do Now assignments, whereas Mrs. Said calls them *Settle In* activities. When students are done with that activity, they are expected to put their devices away, and are welcome to use the various chargers Mrs. Said provides around the room. Next, the entire class engages in a community breath and meditation before reviewing the learning targets for the lesson. When the lesson calls for it, devices are used intentionally, like finding a visual or research. *Sigh*...Mrs. Said's classroom sounds so inviting, don't you think?

You've already read about my identity, and I've asked you to consider how your identity impacts how you present as an educator. In the rest of this chapter, we will spend time thinking about how we can *know what we don't know* about our students so that they do, in fact, know that we care—about their language, culture, interests, and even their hopes and dreams. You might be thinking, *But I'm a secondary teacher with over a hundred students on my total caseload! I'm not working with the same group of students all day like an elementary classroom teacher who gets more time with a smaller group of students. I don't have that kind of time to get to know every single one of my students.* I completely understand; I've been there, and rest assured, I only present to you an array of ideas here that you can choose from that may work for you given your schedule and your rosters of students. Keep in mind, though, that relationship-building can go a long way!

And by the way, elementary teachers may be saying to themselves, *I do have one class all day every day, and I still am not sure how to integrate what I do find out about my students! Help!* Yes, no matter what grade level we are teaching, this is challenging work. Please remember as you go through this chapter that some students may be more challenging to get to know, especially if they are from different cultural and linguistic backgrounds from what you're used to. You may use the ideas presented here for one student or a small number of students you'd like to learn more about. On the other hand, you may decide to try out some of these tips with your whole class. It's really up to you and what is needed and possible in your specific teaching situation. The important thing is to remember that all our students bring assets to the classroom, and it's our job to discover those strengths—to honor our students and engage them in deep learning.

Teach Your Students, Not Just Your Content

Before planning any academic content, it is crucial to get to know our students and try to put ourselves in their shoes. We can have all the latest and greatest teaching strategies in our toolbox, but if we don't stop to get to know our students, we may not get that far in actually advancing their learning. It is important to remember that educators are responsible for meeting students where they are and honoring who they are in their learning experiences. Identities must be examined and valued as we plan learning experiences, including our identities as educators and those of our students. Our mindset matters in our approach to teaching students from all different backgrounds. It is imperative to learn about who our students are and what they bring to our classroom instead of assuming that one way of instruction will work—or should work—for all students. This is particularly important with diverse learners whose cultural and linguistic identities may not be represented in a traditional U.S. school setting.

At Confianza, we teach educators to reflect and deepen what we call an *equity-based mindset* because we want all educators to strive for access, opportunity, and ultimately equitable outcomes for all students. We promote empathy-building and perspective-taking. In this chapter, I will refer to getting to know our students and integrating their backgrounds as *identity investment*. Remember, however, that we cannot fully experience what our students and their families (or anyone else for that matter) experience. Plus, who we are impacts how we see others. Let's exercise curiosity about others' experiences to meet them where *they* are, not where *we* are. Let's build bridges of understanding so that all students experience a sense of belonging in our classrooms.

A Return on Investment

When we take the time to get to know our students and their unique gifts and experiences, we show them that we care about who they are, want to learn about their experiences, and want to hear their stories and voices. We show them that we are investing in them as people and taking the time to integrate their identities into the classroom. When we honor who our students are, we demonstrate that learning is co-constructed, a constant transaction between teacher and students. When we invest in our students' identities, we can experience a return on this investment in the form of increased student engagement and higher performance, not to mention potentially more joyful teaching and learning! In other words, when we see engaged students, we are doing something right (Villalobos, 2020).

More than anything, when we value students' identities, we model the habit of lifelong learning as a member of our learning community, reaping the rewards of learning from our students, something I have become richer for throughout my years of teaching, having worked with hundreds of students from various backgrounds. For every student I have taught, he or she has taught me so much, often things I would never have learned had I been closed to them teaching me. Having been both a classroom teacher and a language specialist, I've learned from all my students and their families. Because of their richly diverse cultural and linguistic backgrounds, I've been able to learn about the world right in my classroom.

Demonstrating Mutual Respect and Trust

It's important to maintain an asset-based mindset and remember that culturally and linguistically diverse students often bring experiences not always recognized by the general education curriculum. That's why our job, as their teachers, is to integrate their identities into the classroom. By doing so, we demonstrate mutual respect and trust by exhibiting that we embrace the diversity within our classrooms. In fact, I named my organization Confianza after this cultural concept. *Confianza* in Spanish means *mutual respect and trust,* which is at the heart of all learning. I came across the word *confianza* when living and working in Spanish-speaking communities. One of the beautiful parts of knowing more than one language is that some words and concepts simply do not translate. Confianza is one of those words!

A big part of the language lens approach is bringing in students' and families' (and educators'!) funds of knowledge. *Funds of knowledge* is a key concept in working with culturally and linguistically diverse students and families (González, Moll, & Amanti, 2005; Moll, 1992). When we incorporate students' funds of knowledge with our students, we enact *confianza*. In this way, we can help make sure that students feel included in the classroom and in charge of their own learning careers. Plus, we might even learn something new about our students, our community, or the world! Ultimately, by more intentionally incorporating of students' home lives or funds of knowledge into our planning, we can hope for a subsequent increase in engagement and overall performance.

A Global and Multicultural Perspective

Often with some students, we may see a disconnection between home and school. One reason is that, aside from the language being a challenge, much of the curriculum may feature topics from the dominant culture and dominant lexicon that may not be readily accessible to learners from other cultures and language groups. For example, when studying literature, science, social studies, and even math, we generally come from a white, Anglo, Western perspective, not necessarily a global one, a multicultural one nor a multilingual one. If we can uncover this mismatch of student experience to the curriculum, we may be able to enhance our curriculum to better match the lives of our students. If our goal is for students to be more engaged in the classroom, doesn't it make sense that their identities are somehow present in it? If students aren't engaged in the curriculum, disenfranchisement, underperformance, not to mention behavior issues, can result. As my esteemed graduate advisor, the late Dr. Martin Haberman at the University of Wisconsin, would always say, *The best classroom management is a student-centered curriculum.* I worked hard in my formative teaching years to make the curriculum more meaningful for my students so that they could see their identities reflected in the classroom and be inspired to contribute, learn, and grow. This is the art of teaching.

My hope here is for you to consider how you invest in your students' identities in order to demonstrate respect for their backgrounds and to provide connections to the topic at hand. The role of the teacher is critical in setting the tone for students and exemplifying safe, respectful learning. By connecting students' lives and their families' lives to the curriculum more intentionally, we can enact a richer learning experience overall. So how do we do this? How can we invest in our students' identities?

First things first, learn to pronounce students' names the way they want to have them pronounced. I recommend that we refrain from assuming we know how names are pronounced. We can simply *ask.* My last name gets mispronounced all the time, so I use a mnemonic device; i*t's* AUTO, *like automobile!* Some educators I work with have the student say their name in a private video or audio clip so that it can be referenced for easy access. Other educators write down how to pronounce names' phonetically in a way that can help them remember. Pronouncing names correctly also applies to the names of siblings, parents, and guardians. People have names, and names represent a big part of people's identities.

Types of English Language Learners

Next, let's discuss who English language learners are. But first, we need to remind ourselves that English language learners, or MLLs, are not a monolithic group. Our multilingual learners come to us with all sorts of language histories, family experiences, and a myriad of other factors affecting how they perform in school. We do want to keep in mind that every child is different in his or her unique ways, yet we can group students, particularly MLLs, into several different types: newcomers, immigrants, refugees, migrants, students with limited or interrupted formal education (often referred to as SLIFE or SIFE), and long-term MLLs. Labeling a group can, however, lead to lower expectations if we see everyone in that group as equal and see the problem as the student, not their circumstances (Hattie, 2023).

Identifying what types of MLLs you have in your class is not always so clear-cut since students have their own unique stories and may fit into several categories—newcomer, refugee, migrant, sojourner, or student with limited or interrupted formal education (SLIFE) (Freeman, & Freeman, 2004). Newcomers are essentially immigrants whose families have left their country of origin, some for reasons outside of their control. Those reasons may include war, political turmoil, poverty, and natural disaster (Salva & Matis, 2017). However, not all newcomers are coming here involuntarily. Some newcomers have federal refugee or asylum status, while others may not, yet they may experience similar histories of leaving their countries for extreme reasons. Migrants move from place to place seeking work, which can lead to gaps in education. Sojourners are typically MLLs who come to a new country on a temporary basis, like a foreign-exchange student or a child whose family has a short-term placement for work. Still, we have students with limited or interrupted formal education, more commonly referred to as SLIFE students. SLIFE MLLs are new to the United States, have limited schooling in their home language, have limited L1 literacy skills (just because one can speak a language does not mean they can read/write in it!), may come to us as unaccompanied minors, and are typically below grade level across all academic skills.

Students in any of these categories may or may not be completely new to the English language and U.S. culture based on their unique experiences. Please note that beginner MLLs at any age are brand new or very new to English and may be in the "silent period" for some time. That means we don't want to force them to speak; we provide lots of support and wait time for them to process between languages. Just think of what they are going through—socially, emotionally, and culturally!

Long-term MLLs are typically U.S.-born students who may appear to speak English proficiently but are generally not proficient with academic language across the content areas, very often in literacy—or reading and writing. Across the country, long-term English learners are an increasing concern for schools due to general underperformance and significant dropout rates compared to their non-MLL peers. As a whole, this group of students can go largely unnoticed in classrooms due to perhaps appearing to be fluent in English conversational skills. Teachers often tell me, "But they sound proficient! How can they still be an English learner?" when, in fact, language development may be fossilized or stuck. We don't want any student to become long-term in their language development. We want to accelerate their language development!

I stress here that being below grade level in literacy for MLLs who are still acquiring English proficiency is a natural part of language acquisition. This means that it's common for long-term MLLs to struggle with reading and writing, which is an expected part of the process. However, this does not mean we ignore or penalize students in this situation; it means we change our instructional practices to better teach them. In many, many cases, improving our literacy strategies across the curriculum is essential for engaging MLLs in content instruction, a set of practices I aspire to integrate for you throughout this book.

• • •

Two Student Stories

To demonstrate how MLLs vary in terms of their backgrounds and how important it is to get to know them individually, allow me to tell you the stories of two different students I've taught. First, we have Liling. Liling came to me in fifth grade as a newcomer MLL from China. Almost immediately, Liling changed her name to the more Americanized Lily, which is not uncommon for students to do to fit into their new culture, albeit a major change to their linguistic and cultural identity. Lily had had some exposure to English in her former school. She had lived with her grandmother from age five until age ten, when her mother sent for her from the United States. Her mother immigrated to the United States before Lily to get settled with a job. Lily's mother had also met a Caucasian man from the U.S. whom she married and who then became Lily's stepfather. When Lily came to her new country, new school, and new language, she was also joining a new family. Can you imagine what Lily was going through?

As the language screener told us upon her arrival, Lily's English proficiency was mainly in reading and writing since her oral language skills were emerging. Also, in talking with her mother, we learned an important cultural factor—Chinese schools taught some English with a stronger focus on literacy than (oracy) speaking and listening skills. It was immediately evident Lily was extremely motivated to learn, as evident by the following text (which was dictated to me in the creation of her identity text using a strategy called the language experience approach [Cummins et al., 2005]):

> My first day of school was great. My teachers talked a lot to me, even though I didn't understand them. I was still grateful. I tried to learn to speak and understand English, but it was too hard, even though I was still strong enough to learn English. Now I am in America for one and half years, after all the hard work I finally understand English, but still a lot more to learn in my life. But my brain or my heart believes that in two years I will be as good as all the kids my age.

Lily was the kind of student who would work overtime to succeed. She worked very hard during school and worked overtime after school and on weekends, telling me again and again that she wanted to "be as good as all the kids" her age. We talked about how English language development is a process, and it takes years. I told her she was already "as good as" the other kids and, in fact, had a stronger brain because she had such strong proficiency in her first language, Mandarin.

Lily wasn't shy about showing her classmates how she used Chinese comic books to improve her English vocabulary. In my one-on-one time teaching Lily, we discussed her previous schooling experience in China. I learned there was a competitive spirit focused on individual achievement, and that cooperative group work was hard for Lily because of this. Her parents and I spoke about her propensity for perfectionism and strategies to expand her awareness to other facets of her life beyond her laser-like focus on her English language development.

Over time, and very quickly compared to other newcomers with strong L1 (first language) proficiency, Lily could more easily express herself both socially and academically in English and transfer her L1 literacy skills to English, even though Mandarin and English have a completely different script system, which is a major factor for academic success when MLLs with home literacy skills actually transfer literacy skills from one language to another. Of note here is that my own experiences of immersing myself in my studies as a means to escape, as I shared with you earlier in this chapter, had an impact on how I perceived Lily, when her high achieving was more about a cultural difference from her Chinese schooling model.

Lily went on to middle school as a confident, strong young woman proud of her English skills and Chinese heritage. She ended up sharing her life story that we created in her identity text with her classroom teacher, who was amazed at all the funds of knowledge that Lily brought to her new school. To learn more about how to try out identity texts, check out resources for family and student engagement at languagelens.com.

Next, we have Martin. I had Martin in my fourth-grade classroom during my second year of teaching. However, at the time, I wasn't yet an MLL teacher and didn't fully understand how to connect with him effectively. Looking back, I often wish I could go back and reteach

Martin and other students like him, armed with the knowledge and skills that I've gained since then. This hindsight has fueled my desire to help other educators who, like me, were content teachers without a language lens.

Martin was a Mexican American student who was very withdrawn and had beginning English-language proficiency. Looking back, I'm honestly not sure if his tendency to withdraw was due to his personality or mostly his status as an MLL, but at any rate, he was very quiet, and I wasn't exactly sure how to engage him. He was flagged as an MLL student but one who was *exiting* or *transitioning* from needing services.

I often felt helpless to provide him what he needed, although I did try my best with the tools I had at the time. Martin and I were successful one-on-one through conversations guided by my asking yes/no and WH questions (who, what, why, where, when, and how). Martin could also communicate his thoughts through writing with enough support—such as using sentence stems and word banks (see Chapter 3 for more about language differentiation strategies)—along with a lot of encouragement and modeling from me. The times that were the most challenging for him to engage were during whole-group instruction. Compounding this issue was that his well-meaning parents did not come to conferences or return my phone calls. This could have been due largely to the language barrier or the fact that the parents worked different shifts. It could have also been due to what I learned from other Mexican American families later on—that, culturally, respect is shown to the school by not getting involved and by allowing *la maestra* (the teacher) to do her work unaided by families.

This cultural difference can easily be misperceived if we come from the dominant cultural assumption that all families should get involved at school the same way. Remember, there's more than one way to engage in school, especially when we are working with families from various backgrounds and languages. Furthermore, as I explained earlier in this chapter, my own parents had been very active in my education and in advocating for the equal education of my sister with disabilities. In this way, my own experience shaped how I perceived the lack of engagement from Martin's parents. Yet, as I learned and continue to learn all the time, different does not mean wrong.

Years later, when teaching an ESL/bilingual education graduate course, I came across this quote, which starkly reminded me of Martin. It is something I imagine he might have said to himself in my classroom:

> Sometimes I would try to look like I knew what was going on; sometimes I would just try to think about a happy time when I didn't feel stupid. My teacher never called on me or talked to me. I think they either forgot I was there or else wished I wasn't. (Ovando & Combs, 2012, p. 13)

Certainly, I never wished Martin wasn't in my class. Yet I could tell he was struggling, and he was aware of how much he was struggling in comparison to the other students. Worse yet, I didn't fully know how to bridge that gap. I wasn't bridging to his home language of Spanish by capitalizing on the similarities between English and Spanish (i.e., teaching cognates to Martin and other Spanish-speaking students, like *nation* and *nación*). A cognate is a word that has a shared root across languages. I wasn't figuring out Martin's learning profile to make an effective differentiation plan for him, nor was I able to provide ways to engage him in the whole group. As painful as this memory is for me as his teacher, can you imagine what Martin was going through? And can we imagine what he went through yet? How many other Martins are there?

Putting Ourselves in Students' Shoes

As we will keep returning to this guide, it is important to start with students and try to put ourselves in their shoes, figuratively speaking. We first need to start with where *we* are as educators, and also start with where *our learners* are and who they are. We need to learn all we can about them to reach them more effectively. Because MLLs come to us with all sorts of language histories and other factors affecting achievement, it can be very helpful to learn their language histories, as

I have presented here with Lily and Martin. As previously stated, MLLs are not a monolithic group. However, understanding the types or ways we can group MLLs with similar language backgrounds can be very useful, even though we still want to remember that every child is different.

Lily was a newcomer, a student new to the United States. In contrast, Martin was not a newcomer MLL but a U.S.-born, Spanish-speaking Latino who fit in the MLL category of long-term English learner, or LTEL, MLL student "at risk" of not graduating. At exceptionally high risk are Hispanic students. While graduation rates have increased in the past ten years, Hispanic students have higher dropout rates than other major racial and ethnic groups (Fry, 2014). Plus, LTELs are an increasing subgroup of concern due to their underperformance and significant dropout rates (Bear & McEvoy, 2015). LTELs can be speakers of Spanish or other language groups. Yet, as a whole, this group of students—like Martin—can go largely unnoticed in classrooms due to minimal participation in class and appearing to be fluent in English conversational skills.

Tan Huyhn and Beth Skelton caution us to watch our language, saying that the term LTEL is a deficit-based, structural barrier that keeps students in a "negative whirlpool of low expectations" that include remedial classes and barriers to advanced classes in secondary school (para. 6, Ellevation Education, 2023). I could not agree more. We need to update our language to update our understanding. As I explained at the start of this chapter, I myself was labeled an "at risk" high school student when that label really didn't tell the whole story, nor did it do any favors for my self-esteem or my teachers' mindsets of me. We can ask students to share how they identify themselves, not identify them fully for them.

Language Proficiency Levels

In order to know our students, we need to understand their language history and their language levels. Historically, we referred to the process of learning another language as second language acquisition. I believe that term is very much out of date since many of the

MLLs I've taught were learning English as an additional language, whether it be second, third, fourth, or more!

You may already know this, but many other countries are bilingual and multilingual, with the United States being primarily composed of monolinguals, although even that statistic is rapidly changing. Of note is that the United States does not have an official language (although some of the U.S. states do), although there has been a historical push to adopt one; check out the articles on dual language/biliteracy at languagelens.com further your learning on linguistic history in the United States.

Also of note is that the field of education uses a variety of acronyms to describe language and its learners. In my travels supporting Confianza's partner schools throughout the United States and internationally, I see all these acronyms at play:

- MLL: English language learners
- EL: English learners
- ESL: English as a second language
- ESOL: English for speakers of other languages
- EAL: English as an additional language
- ENL: English as a new language
- DLL: dual language learners
- MLL: multilingual language learners
- Emerging bilingual students
- Simultaneous bilinguals

It's important to know that what we call this group of students can largely depend on what state, system, or country we're in, what program we work in, and what policies we follow. Yes, know your local acronym, but more than anything, please try to stay focused on the fact that no matter what you call English language learners, this group of students is comprised of students from diverse backgrounds with unique needs and so much to teach us. They all go through the process of acquiring a language as a new language! We hope that they all make it through every stage of the process, but unfortunately, as I discussed earlier in this chapter, like Martin, many do not, mainly because the system isn't adequately designed to meet their needs. You see, Martin's underachievement was not a within-child issue; it was a failure within the system.

At any rate, the process of learning a new language is pretty universal and, as you can see in Figure 2.2, can be summarized into the following five stages (TESOL, 2006; Freeman, Freeman, & Mercuri, 2002; Krashen & Terrell, 1983), although check your local system for the exact labels your school uses. In this guidebook, I will chunk these levels together into the following proficiency bands shown in Figure 2.2 to make grouping more manageable as you start to differentiate students' needs by language: Beginner: approximately levels 1–2; Intermediate: approximately levels 3–4; Advanced: approximately levels 4–5.

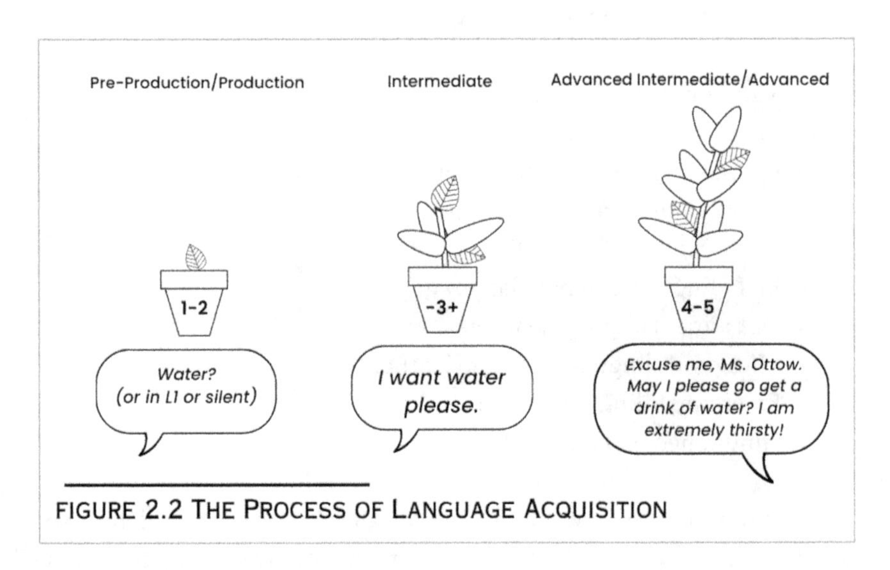

FIGURE 2.2 THE PROCESS OF LANGUAGE ACQUISITION

The figure text indicates a student asking the teacher (in this case, me, Ms. Ottow) for a drink of water. I use the student request to ask for a drink of water as the touchpoint here throughout the stages for two reasons. First, it's a common question, yet it's one that a student might not realize how difficult it is to ask in a new language as compared to his or her first language. Second, asking for a drink of water is a social language task. Social language can be somewhat easier for students to learn because it's everywhere—spoken by teachers, by other students, on the playground, in the community, and so on. Please note that students' home language may be in full bloom, yet we may only see their English development as Figure 2.1 illustrates. Keep in mind, though, that this illustration of the plants shows the development of English language acquisition. Like each plant has roots beneath the surface, so does each multilingual learner in their own home language or languages.

Asking for a drink of water is one task a student may do at school and it's under the umbrella of social language. The delineation here is the academic language of content classrooms, which is the tougher stuff. Academic language is what we teach alongside social language in our content classrooms. You might be thinking, *Well, how do I know what my MLLs can do at different stages using academic language?* That's a great question that we will dive into in the following chapters. For now, I'd like to ensure you get this overview of the general developmental sequences students go through when adding an additional language.

Not all students with the same overall proficiency level have the same needs or strengths. Be aware, as we will discuss in Chapter 4, that students use four domains of language—reading, writing, listening, and speaking— and not every student develops all four domains at the same rate! Although these levels above are somewhat general and universal, again, please consult your local language proficiency level resources and policies for the precise terminology and levels used in your unique setting. Plus, it's advisable to consult your MLL specialist to get the most current language development data about your MLLs, since students' proficiency levels can differ across each domain to comprise their overall composite level. And if you don't have MLLs, try to relate to the other takeaway here: language is complex and there's more than meets the eye for MLLs and ALLs!

I find that those of us who speak English as our first language don't really know the nuances of language as well as those who successfully make it through the stages as MLLs. Again, we can take English for granted, and underestimate how challenging it really is. That's why we want to scaffold for our language learners, more for the beginning stages and less for those at the advanced stages. However, as we have discussed, scaffolds accommodate the content, so often times specific scaffolds work for ALL learners.

Sequential versus Simultaneous Bilinguals

Of note is that while we can assign *types* to our very diverse MLL students, these bilingual or multilingual students can present with two different linguistic profiles. As dual language specialist D. García (2018) explains, we have sequential bilinguals and simultaneous bilinguals. First, the sequential bilingual has a defined proficiency in his or her home language (L1) before adding an additional language. I am a sequential bilingual because I've learned and keep learning other languages at varying proficiency levels, adding to my first language, English. The second kind of linguistic profile is the simultaneous bilingual. Simultaneous bilinguals are not yet fossilized in one language before adding another language. These learners operate in two or more languages across different contexts and use two or more languages to negotiate meaning in various spaces with different audiences. Cummins (2017) offers another view to contrast additive versus subtractive models of bilingualism with the term *active bilingualism* that "endorses the…the understanding that languages are intertwined in complex ways in the minds of multilingual individuals," and that schools need to not just teach students how to connect their languages but also "challenge the operation of raciolinguistic ideologies, and societal power relations more broadly, as an essential condition for reversing patterns of underachievement among minoritized students" (p. 406).

Sadly, I've witnessed many students of all ages actually lose proficiency in their heritage language, thus resulting in *subtractive bilingualism*. This is when speakers of a language trade their *mother tongue* for English-only. On a macro level, globally, we are experiencing the erasure of languages on a massive scale; one language dies or ceases to be used on Earth every two weeks (Rymer, 2012). When working with your students and their families, please keep in mind that there are many reasons why loss of the home language can occur, so please work with the student and their family/guardians/caretakers in understanding the student's unique story, which includes their language history, language preferences, and language goals. In the two student stories I've presented in this chapter, Lily was a sequential bilingual, while Martin was a simultaneous bilingual. Building on students' linguistic strengths is key in classrooms, while not deemphasizing the linguistic gifts that bilingualism and multilingualism bring (García, 2018).

Students with Disabilities

For students who are dually identified as MLLs with disabilities, Samuels (2021) asserts that we must adhere to "an equity-driven learning space that makes them feel valued while learning" (para. 2). Many IEPs only mandate accommodations of the instruction, not completely different content standards. However, some students with significant disabilities may require modified standards that are different from those of their peer cohort. Please refer to your local special education department for specific students' Individualized Education Plans (IEPs). These plans outline specific goals and support strategies designed to help these students achieve their unique learning objectives. As such, it's important to plan your instruction accordingly to ensure that these students are making progress up the mountain, which may or may not be the same mountain other students are on. It really depends on that specific student's learning support plan.

In my consulting work with schools that teach multilingual students with visual impairments and students who are deaf and hard of hearing, I have been illuminated by these educators' experiences, some of whom also have disabilities like their students themselves. In this space, I have learned some important statistics about multilingual deaf and heard of hearing (DHH) students, which I will share with you here. Over 23% of DHH students are also MLLs, and over 30% of students in this group are Latino (Gerner de García, 2013). Students with visual impairments (VI) who are MLL students are not just learning content and a new language but also the language of braille. Students who are deafblind and identify as multilingual require not just linguistically responsive instruction like this guidebook outlines plus braille (Ellen, n.d.) plus what is now emerging, as some linguists argue, as a sign language specifically for the deafblind (Leland, 2022). Language sure is fluid, and adapts to the needs of the people who use it.

Physical impairments are the most common kinds of disabilities in the U.S. (Martinez, 2022). For me personally, watching my sister with physical disabilities adapt herself to an able-bodied society throughout my life impresses me. Yet within the adult population, over 25% of us have some kind of disability which can be any impairment that affects our vision, movement, thinking, remembering, learning, communicating, hearing, mental health, and social relationships (Centers for Disease Control and Prevention, 2020). Let's not forget that some disabilities can present as "invisible," which means they only present themselves when barriers come up. For example, I have been recently diagnosed with two autoimmune diseases, which only become apparent to onlookers when I'm around food. If I ingest certain ingredients, my body starts attacking itself, triggering multiple, complex medical issues. I need to take certain medications for the rest of my life, and my diseases have no cure. No fun for a foodie, I tell you!

It goes without saying, but I'll remind you that disabilities affect people from all walks of life, and *ableism* is when prejudice or discrimination occurs because of one's disability or disabilities. Please consider the language we use around disabilities so that our language is not perpetuating a historical perception that disabilities are deficits. I've recently come to understand that the term *neurodivergent* is an asset-based way of describing people on the autism spectrum, those with neurological or developmental conditions like ADHD or learning disabilities (Baumer & Frueh, 2021). Using words like *insane, crazy,* and *lazy* to describe people are part of an ableist paradigm (Ravishankar, 2020). We can try terms like *differently-abled* and *neurotypical.* Language is fluid because our culture is always changing!

Just like our language lens can urge us to question a paradigm that implies that English is somehow superior to other languages, which is not at all true, we can also use our language lens to question any paradigm that implies that one group is somehow superior to another.

I'm working on removing these ableist terms from my vocabulary because these words have been used to describe people with mental illness in a derogatory way. I also hold sacred asset-based language and equity-based language, which I will explain more in depth below. Not only have I experienced mental health issues myself, but a big part of my childhood had me defending my younger sister with physical disabilities and learning disabilities from hurtful words like *retard* and *flatface*. Words do matter. Language matters. What we say and what we allow as people in positions of influence can make a major difference for even just one student or a group of students. Take stock of your language and how it may be unintentionally hurting others. With your language lens, I encourage you to ask others to do the same.

The Role of Culture in Learning (and in Life!)

As we get clear about what general types of students we are working with, we should also analyze the role of culture. A common and helpful metaphor for understanding the myriad cultural factors is an iceberg. What we see above the surface are the surface-level components of culture—food, dress, language, celebrations, and the arts. However, the majority of a culture is what we can't see, and those components exist below the surface—unspoken rules, like how a culture enacts body language, concepts about time, nonverbal communication, and personal space. Still, deeper parts of a culture are even further below the surface. They can often be totally invisible, yet when contrasted with a new culture, the differences can be stark and the similarities surprising. Examples of deeper culture are attitudes toward aged relatives, ideas of parenting, family structures, preference for competition versus cooperation, how we use eye contact, and roles in relation to gender, age, and career. While it is important to know what's visible about a student's or family's culture (e.g., language, cultural traditions), please remember that what we don't see, or what is invisible, also defines that culture. Even with the best intentions, if we only focus on the tip of the proverbial iceberg, we may rely on a limited perception of a culture and even stereotype a cultural group. If we want to understand these deeper factors, we must go beyond what we can't always see and get to know what we don't know.

Culture Shock

In thinking about how students' culture affects learning, let's not underestimate the impact of culture shock. Culture shock is the disorientation that occurs when a person moves to a new or different cultural environment. Some describe it in four stages: honeymoon, where everything is fun and new; shock, when differences become clearer and frustration can set in; gradual adjustment, when you find ways to cope; and acculturation, when you start to feel more integrated and even at home.

When I was a young teacher who moved from Wisconsin to Puerto Rico in my mid-twenties, I experienced these stages of culture shock over the first eight months I was there. At first, everything was magical and exciting. *I can quickly learn more Spanish! I love salsa dancing! What a beautiful island!* Then after a while, things got hard. In new situations, I couldn't always remember basic Spanish grammatical structures, and I sometimes felt like I spoke like a five-year-old in my second language. I became disoriented and exhausted easily. I wasn't picking up on subtle nonverbal culture cues that conveyed a deeper meaning. I became frustrated. Over time, I found ways to adapt, ensuring I had "English brain breaks" with my *Norteamericano*/North American friends. I was reminded by many folks I met from nations across the Caribbean, Central America, and South America that the terms *America* and *Americans* were viewed as ethnocentric since *America* is a geographic region that is the entire Western Hemisphere, not just one country with the name *The United States of America.* Over almost two years on the island, I became more bilingual and somewhat bicultural! Although I was an adult *voluntary* language learner, it really stuck with me what it must be like to be from a non-U.S. culture and non-English-language background for many of our *nonvoluntary* language learner students and their families.

• • •

Factors Affecting School Performance

When designing an instructional program or any interaction with our MLL students, we need to take the time to get to know them and what unique assets and challenges they bring to school. By uncovering what factors affect their success, we can more adequately meet their needs while honoring their stories and our cultural responsiveness. Major factors that affect academic success for MLLs include but are not limited to the following (WIDA, 2013):

- Age
- Strengths and interests
- L1 literacy skills and home language usage
- Schooling history, including interrupted schooling and cultural value of L1 schooling experience
- Differences and similarities between l1 and english
- Responsibilities with family
- Family and cultural values about education
- Trauma or other stress that can block learning in the brain

The process of getting to know our students is complex yet paramount to effective MLL schooling. These factors affecting school success may be below the surface and shed some light on ways to build on strengths. Instead of focusing on what is on the surface and, thus, maybe only looking at what is not working, in this critical part of the planning process, I offer ideas to go deeper by getting to know your students' backgrounds to move toward a more multicultural and multilingual mindset.

The Intersectionality of Race and Language

Over 90% of our MLLs are students of color (National Center for Education Statistics, 2019). During the coronavirus pandemic, BIPOC (Black, Indigenous, and People of Color) were disproportionately affected by the virus and other symptoms of systemic racism, including lack of access to adequate medical care, increased unemployment, and pervasive poverty. Latino children were eight times, and

Black children were five times more likely than their white peers to be hospitalized with COVID-19 (Centers for Disease Control and Prevention, 2021). Underlying inequities that were indeed in place before the pandemic continue as the pandemic wanes and seemingly ends. Therefore, I recommend that, as educators working in diverse communities, we continuously look inward to our personal biases as social agents both at the classroom and systems levels. As I discussed in Chapter 1, the *mainstream* model doesn't work for everyone because it often reflects a white, monolingual view that does not include all groups. As Rosa and Flores (2021) explain, it's not about individuals being malicious, per se, but it's about stepping back and questioning historically established structural institutions like assessments and grouping language learners and/or students of color as inherently *deficient* or needing remediation.

As educators, to get students to be ready to learn, we need to examine who our students are, across all identity groups—race, ethnicity, class, language, religious affiliation, gender identity, sexual orientation, ability, immigration status—and understand the *intersectionality* of belonging to multiple groups. We need to integrate social-emotional learning and come to the classroom with a more holistic view of who our students are and how they can learn to their potential.

During the COVID pandemic, we collectively noticed that we were moving into a *new normal.* Well, let's face it; the *old* normal did not work for everyone anyways. Let's move forward into a space where all students feel respected, accepted, encouraged, and included in the classroom. When we make belonging a central part of classrooms, we are, in fact, fostering a powerful precursor to learning (Hattie, 2023). *This is the new mainstream.* Let's not make assumptions about our students or about each other but take the time to invest in each other's identities for inclusive, stronger communities going forward.

Student Data Dive

To get a more holistic view of a student's story, go below the surface of traditional measures like achievement tests and demographics. Figure 2.3 shows how you can sketch out these factors to systematically learn about a student in the form of a Student Data Dive. Here, we learn about a student named Jaspreet. She is an amalgam of several students I've had the honor of teaching and part of several Sikh families I've had the pleasure of knowing over the years. When I do a dive on students, I like to include artifacts like I've done here, a real drawing from a former student who was teaching me (and her classmates) about her faith and what specific items of the Sikh religious culture signify. Plus, a picture can speak a thousand words! The important thing is to build *confianza* with students and their families so that bridges of understanding and learning can be formed. There's so much to know underneath the surface!

Please remember that we don't learn everything about a student overnight. And sometimes we don't learn all we need to despite our best efforts of getting to know the student and their family or guardian. But we can try in our effort to invest in their identity. If you'd like more ideas on creating a plan for individual students or groups of students, look through the resources for data and assessment at languagelens.com.

Student Name & Grade	Jaspreet, 8th grade
Language Background	Speaks Punjabi and had some exposure to English literacy in India prior to arrival in US; She is a Newcomer to the U.S. Overall, Jaspreet is a Beginner MLL with some emerging Intermediate skills; Stronger in oral language versus reading/writing
Strengths	She is very proud of her Sikh culture and goes to her *gurdwara* regularly. She seems motivated and (more and more) volunteers in class after she has practiced the concept and the target language. She is very social and able to converse with peers socially in English and use social media fluently!
Other Factors	Note that her extended family travels back to India every February so prepare work accordingly as an accommodation. Jaspreet is a very proud big sister to Harbinder, who is starting Kindergarten next year.

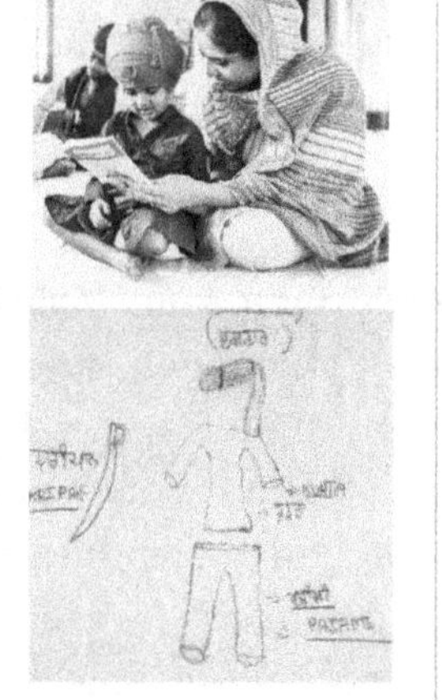

FIGURE 2.3 SAMPLE STUDENT DATA DIVE

Building versus Activating Background Knowledge

This chapter focuses largely on getting to know students so that we can honor their identities and integrate them into our content classroom. When we launch a unit or a lesson, we need to connect to students' backgrounds to hook them into the learning and see what they know or don't know about the topic. Often I hear teachers say, *That student doesn't have any background knowledge.* Well, that is simply not true. Every learner comes with something. Language theorist and researcher Jim Cummins (2010) says, "*No learner is a blank slate*" (p. 21). We may have students in front of us who don't have a direct experience with the concept at hand, in which case we do actually need to *build* background. On the other hand, we may have a learner in front of us who actually does have experience with the topic at hand but isn't able to share that due to a language barrier or because the learner doesn't have adequate access to what we are presenting. In this case, we need to *activate* their background knowledge.

Like a plant with vast roots below the surface, we need to consider that our students may already have the funds of knowledge to connect to what we are teaching. Assuming that they don't, even with the best of intentions, can underestimate students' existing knowledge, skills, and experiences and, in turn, disenfranchise them from their own learning process. No deficit thinking or deficit language! For examples of how you can interrupt deficit attitudes, see the resources on leading for equity at languagelens.com.

Multicultural and Multilingual Mindset

It's important to keep an asset-based mindset and remember that many students often bring experiences that aren't always seen in the traditional curriculum and that it's our job, as their teachers, to integrate their identities into the classroom. By getting to know our students better, we may see a disconnection between home culture and school culture. This disconnect can contribute to root issues of underperformance for bilingual learners in that the minorities are expected to adjust or assimilate to the dominant culture, as opposed to a more *cultural pluralist* approach (Baker, 2014). In schools, cultural pluralism, in contrast to assimilation, looks like true multicultural education that goes beyond the status quo or simply celebrates heroes and holidays or minority cultures to ensure that all schooling practices provide equity for all groups. As we have discussed, a big part of this is getting to know students and the factors that affect their learning. Another way is to incorporate their actual home languages into our classroom.

Incorporating Languages

We have discussed the types of MLLs and the factors of language and culture in learning. The role of the home language, heritage language, or mother tongue—which we will call L1—is paramount to learning for multilingual populations. Generally speaking, the stronger students' L1 is, the more easily and efficiently they can transfer skills to English/L2. However, as discussed previously in regard to sequential versus simultaneous bilinguals, we need to know if they have oral language skills in their L1 and/or if they also have literacy skills in their L1. It can be hard to know precise information about L1 without an L1 language assessment in reading, writing, listening, and speaking, but it's not impossible. You can work with the school staff, like your staff in your Family Welcome Center or your language specialist who has conducted a home language survey, which is federally required in all U.S. schools as part of the identification process for MLLs. This document can be a starting point for learning language history. Please remember that some students are learning English as a third or fourth language, so they may have an L2, an L3 . . . not just a second language. As I mentioned earlier, because languages other than English can be viewed as *inferior* and many languages are even disappearing off the planet, I invite you to see your role as a social agent to honor and value all languages.

How do we incorporate students' home language or heritage language (L1) into our classrooms? Incorporating this critical resource is a research-based best practice for teaching MLLs; for many students, clarifying a concept in L1 can be very useful (Echevarria, Vogt, & Short, 2017). Even if we don't have a bilingual program model, we can still bring in students' L1. Even if you don't speak another language besides English, you can still honor other languages in your classroom! For many students with a base in L1, clarifying a concept in L1 can be very useful. Even if we don't have a bilingual program model, we can still bring in students' L1 to show that it is valued. However, please understand that not every MLL has oral language or literacy skills in their L1, so please get to know more about their skills whenever possible.

Figure 2.4 shows an example greetings anchor chart in different languages. It's based on a group of students I taught who spoke four different languages besides English—Korean, Spanish, Polish, and Hindi. Note in the chart that there is a flag from Puerto Rico *and* the Dominican Republic for this particular group of students. The students and their families helped create it. We discussed how there are many ways to greet people depending on the informality or formality, or register, of the interaction. You see, translation is not enough! In this particular classroom, we added new languages to our anchor chart as new students joined us, and the multilingual students really enjoyed being the teachers! Earlier in my career, when I was a monolingual teacher in a bilingual/dual language program (and before I lived in Latin America and became more proficient in Spanish), my students got such a kick out of hearing me speak Spanish. They would say, *Ms. Ottow's learning another language, too!* The class could collectively earn a few minutes on Friday afternoons called, *Teach Ms. Ottow Spanish.* Because my students were from many different backgrounds, we had hot debates about pronunciation and how to say terms and figures of speech across different Spanish dialects.

English	Korean	Spanish	Polish	Hindi
Hello!	안녕하세요! (annyeong haseyo)	Hola (o-lah)	Cześć! (chech-sh-ch)	नमस्ते! (na-mas-te)
How are you?	어떻게 지내셨어요? (eotteoke jinaesyeosseoyo)	¿Cómo estás? (como estas)	Jak się masz? (yak-shay-mash)	आप कैसे हैं? (aap kaise hain)
Thank you.	고마워. (go-ma-wo)	Gracias. (gra-see-as)	Dziękuję. (jen-koo-yea)	धन्यवाद। (dhan-ya-vaad)

FIGURE 2.4 GREETINGS IN MULTIPLE LANGUAGES

Translanguaging

In the multilingual brain, we process using a mix of languages representing our linguistic experience. Please note that throughout English learners' language development process, students often operate in a place of their own personal translanguaging where they are drawing from their own working knowledge of the languages in their purview (García, 2018; Grosjean, 2016; Otheguy, García, & Reid, 2015). Translanguaging means that students live between and within two languages, and they cognitively draw from their language repertoire to make sense of their world. In other words, language learners don't necessarily switch between "channels" per se—the "English channel" or the "Vietnamese channel" when thinking and communicating—but instead use their linguistic resources available to receive and produce ideas. Multilingual people make full use of all language at their fingertips, so to speak, not just what society or contexts tell them to use. This means it's even more crucial to honor and integrate all languages!

I've found tremendous success in my own teaching, and I've seen it in the teaching of many others when we go out on a limb and learn key words and phrases in the languages of our students. Becoming a language learner yourself, if only for a moment, shows students that you appreciate their translanguaging process, care about their language identity, and are also a risk-taker who makes mistakes! One of the best compliments I can receive from both students I've taught and educators I've trained/coached is, *Wow! I love that you are multilingual too! Just like me! Anyone* can learn another language or, at the least, basic greetings in the languages of members of one's community. For more information and practical guidance on translanguaging techniques, see the resources on this topic at languagelens.com in the dual language/biliteracy category.

The Affective Filter

Speaking of risk-taking, we want students to feel comfortable taking risks in our classroom. Language acquisition researcher theorist Stephen Krashen (1986) asserts that emotions play a huge part in learning a language, which in and of itself is full of risks. Krashen refers to the *affective filter* as a mental block to learning that can be affected by the learners' self-confidence, anxiety level, and overall motivation to learn (as cited in Schütz, 2017). Teachers have a lot of influence over the conditions within a classroom and set students up for success. Therefore, we have some influence over a child's affective filter as he or she learns in our classroom. If a classroom is stressful and not conducive to language acquisition, the filter may go up. Then learning is slowed or may not occur at all. If a classroom provides a welcoming space with supportive conditions to learn, the filter may go down, and the students may be in a flow state, motivated to learn and grow. So think about how much your words and actions matter for students' brains to be ready to learn, ready to grow, and ready to reach their potential.

Student Identity Investment

Getting to know students can occur in various ways. A few minutes before or after class or before or after school, a hallway conversation, even having lunch, if possible, to have a simple "getting to know you better" conversation. Perhaps a school-sponsored interpreter is available to allow the student to express themself better if the child is at the beginning stages of English language proficiency. Another great way to learn more about your MLLs and all students in your class is to start the school year or the semester with interest inventories, peer interviews, and/or family interviews. Many teachers I know at all grade levels use these strategies to build a welcoming and inclusive classroom culture that taps into students' backgrounds and interests. Visiting the communities where your students live can be helpful, if possible, to see and hear where they are coming from. In addition, you may also want to consider mapping out the various factors that affect the identities of your MLLs as follows:

- While we don't want to lump individuals into monolithic categories or stereotype people, it can be helpful to see trends and patterns within our student subgroups. Figure out what *type or types* of MLLs you have—newcomers, immigrants, refugees, migrants, sojourners, students with limited or interrupted formal education (SLIFE), and long-term MLLs (LTELs). Do you have dually identified students? Work with your language specialist and special education teacher to learn more about your students and integrate their diversity into your classroom.
- Get information about students' and families' language history, home literacy skills, and literacy practices in their first language. Take time to work with families, especially on intake and during conferences. Listen more than talk. Use interpreters and remind *all* families that they have the right to get information in their home language(s).
- Consider the other factors that affect academic success for English learners as you get to know them, including strengths and interests, schooling history, role in the family and community, family and cultural values about education, and trauma or other stressors that block learning. Think about how you can learn about students' interests and

stories through interest inventories, surveys, interviews, or projects.

- Have representation of the languages in your classroom on the walls through signs and posters (students can help!). You can also learn key phrases and greetings in students' home languages. A little risk-taking on your part can go a long way in showing students that you are trying to understand their experience of learning a new language.
- Provide access and time to clarify key concepts in the classroom in L1 and encourage bilingual dictionaries, including student-made ones, to support language transfers for students who have proficiency in their L1. Encourage metalinguistic awareness by teaching students *contrastive analysis activities* (tasks where students can build bridges between languages). For example, highlight connections between the target language to other languages, including key vocabulary and idioms. Make sure students are doing the heavy lifting; translation alone is not enough!
- When embarking on a new unit of study, research ahead of time to connect the themes or concepts to students' experiences, and consider asking students to incorporate their cultural perspectives.
- Invite students' home practices and / or their families into curricular experiences, tapping into their funds of knowledge to share multicultural math, games, storytelling, food, celebrations, and connections to the curriculum.
- Also, please be sure that interpreters and translations are available for all home languages, and families know these resources exist. The right to interpreters for oral language and to translations for written language is a civil right for all multilingual families in the United States.
- Consider making multilingual videos (or have students make videos!), taking newcomer viewers on a guided tour of the school community.

Remember, taking even some of these steps to show that you invest in your students can pay off significant dividends in terms of relationships and more meaningful learning. You may still be thinking, as we discussed at the beginning of this chapter, *But I have a huge number of students in my class/classes. How can I possibly try all these tips to incorporate everyone's identities?* Well, while you may not be able to learn as much as you want about *every* student, you can target priority students to more effectively connect with them. You may know other staff members, especially language specialists, social workers, and guidance counselors, who can help you do some respectful detective work to learn more about students' backgrounds. Once you have an idea of your students' stories and the factors impacting their learning, you can consider how you are integrating their identities and backgrounds into your teaching.

Going Beyond Asset-Based Language to Equity-Based Language

As part of your language lens, I'd like to invite you to not just embrace asset-based language and thinking but *equity-based* language and thinking. To show you what I mean, consider the differences between these three statements about the same student:

1. *Jorge doesn't have any background knowledge or skills in math. It's impossible to reach him, and he's lazy.*
2. *Let me try to see what math knowledge I can activate and build on with Jorge. Also, what motivates him?*
3. *What blind spot or bias might I have that leads me to believe that Jorge has no background knowledge when that's not true about any learner?*

Sentence #1 is extremely deficit-based. Not only that, but the word *lazy* is considered derogatory because, here, it places a value on Jorge *himself as a person,* not on his *behaviors*. The term *lazy* can stigmatize people as an ableist term and not truly address the root cause of disengagement. As Pollack (2017) states, "What we say about students' abilities and potential shapes how students feel about themselves and how adults offer students opportunities to learn" (p. 127). Language matters, so let's focus on the students' behaviors and seek to understand why their behaviors impede their readiness to learn. If we use absolutes like *doesn't have any, none, never,* and *always,* we minimize the human nuances students bring to the classroom. We aren't using actual evidence to support the student, just judgment.

Let's look at the other two sentences. Sentence #2 is asset-based. Here, we aren't blaming the student, instead, we are looking more expansively into what skills Jorge may bring and what factors may be influencing Jorge's motivation. We see motivation as a *within system/classroom* issue, not a *within child* issue. We are not *otherizing* him but humanizing him. In other words, nothing is wrong with Jorge. The question becomes, *What is wrong with the learning environment? How can we improve what we do to reach Jorge?*

Sentence #3 is—you guessed it--the equity-based version because we go towards self-inquiry to analyze our thinking. We consider that we ourselves have the solution if we only remember that Jorge comes with strengths that our biases may overshadow. Here's another example from a school I've supported with SLIFE students. Instead of framing their English Language Development class as such, the name was *Leadership Academy,* where the students learned English by choosing current events to study and debate each other. What an equity-based approach!

All in all, getting to know our students is complex yet paramount to effective MLL schooling. These factors affecting school success may be below the surface and when we get to know those factors, they can shed some light on ways to build on students' strengths. Through the ideas presented in this chapter, I offer you the chance to go deeper by getting to know your students' strengths and backgrounds so you can integrate key pieces of who they are into your lesson planning and overall pedagogical approach. Be aware, though, that with our new learning about being culturally responsive, educators can feel come some awkwardness or awareness that Zaretta Hammond (2015) refers to as "conscious incompetence" (p. 153). It's okay to be in a state of *I don't know what I don't know.* It's okay to realize that we, as educated educators, may not be fully *up to speed* on how to effectively get to know our diverse learners or how to integrate who they are into our classrooms. We also need not to stereotype students or their families but move towards more multicultural, democratic schooling that includes all. The important thing, however, is to start the process of being more culturally and linguistically responsive, and you can start today!

~

TIPS FOR TEACHERS: HOW DO WE CENTER THOSE STUDENTS IN OUR CLASSROOMS WHO MAY BE ON THE MARGINS?

1. Explore how you identify yourself and what parts of your complex identity impact how you interact with students and teach. Create your own identity wheel and show it to your students as you encourage them to make their own. What is seen? What is unseen? How do we identify ourselves? How do others identify us? See the resources on family and student engagement and leading for equity at languagelens.com.

2. Do you have an MLL or ALL student who would benefit from more identity investment from you? What other staff members may be able to provide you with additional information about their stories? Can you complete a student data dive of this student's story? If you don't know the full story yet, how can you learn more about the student's stories and what factors may impact learning over time? See more resources for student data at languagelens.com.

3. What opportunities may exist in your units and lessons where you can tap into students' linguistic and cultural backgrounds? Are there topics you can explicitly connect to students' experiences, and how might you do that? How can you gauge student engagement to see if doing more identity investment makes a difference?

• • •

4. Are there ways you can collaborate with your content team members, your language specialist, and/or a coach to bring students' identities into your classroom? Here are some ideas to do on your own or with a team:

5. Review your class lists(s) or rosters of students with a language lens. If you don't have language proficiency levels for your MLLs, find them and put them on your list.

6. Make a list of your students grouped into beginner, intermediate, and advanced language proficiency bands. You can also discover which of your students are sequential bilingual or multilingual learners and who may be simultaneous bilingual or multilingual learners. These steps will help you and your team get a general sense of the range of English language needs in your classroom.

7. Consider how you make groups of students and if you could create heterogeneous groups so that MLLs have language models through working with ALLs and/or MLLs at higher proficiency levels.

8. You can also review your students' cultural backgrounds, including national, ethnic, and racial backgrounds, to ensure you know more about the diversity in your classroom. Reflect on whom you call on and when during whole-group discussion and how cultural and/or language may come into play.

~

TIPS FOR COACHES AND LEADERS: HOW CAN ALL LEARNERS' IDENTITIES BE AFFIRMED AS PART OF AN EQUITABLE LEARNING CULTURE?

1. Go back to the Tips for Teachers above. Read #1 above. Show your team and your staff how you identify yourself in order to model how important this process is as social agents in schools. Point out that we can choose to reinforce the status quo, we can choose to keep our cultural blind spots blind, or we can choose to interrupt the status quo and reveal our blind spots through the process of ongoing self-examination, striving to lead towards our vision of equitable schooling. Resources at languagelens.com about leading for equity can help, too.

2. To examine what inequities may exist in your school, take a data dive at student groups. Look for disproportionality and address it. For example, suppose we have an overrepresentation of multilingual learners in intervention and/or Special Education programming. In that case, we may need to look closer at within-system issues to make sure we are not perpetuating inequities in our school. While you're at it, look at the disproportionality between the special education and MLL departments as staffing relates to student caseload. For example, could MLL staffing be increased to provide more equitable access to students? Check out the data and assessment resources at languagelens.com for extra support.

3. Make a more comprehensive data dive a periodic and sacred event at your school. Value multiple measures of data. Use this data to drive your professional learning and program improvements. See the resources on data and assessment at languagelens.com for more on this topic.

- For example, analyze demographic data to see what groups are underrepresented in gifted and talented programs or AP classes.

- Also, use perceptual data sources like student engagement surveys and focus groups of students and families to unearth some sources of disenfranchisement. For instance, in talking to students in classroom observations, I often hear that kids like certain ways teachers teach compared to others. *Out of the mouths of babes,* as they say, can come helpful information and truth we may be unable to see. For student and family input, be sure you include representatives from all groups in your school community.
- If political maelstroms whirl around you and your school community, keep the focus on students. As educators, we may face specific kinds of books being banned and specific kinds of topics being taught. However, our job is to keep all students safe, and make sure all students have a safe environment to feel valued and learn. Don't lose sight of the fact that we are here to include and support ALL students; nothing is political about that.
- Consider creating a community portrait to really understand what identity groups are represented in your school and families. For example, you may find that your Hispanic/Latino/Latinx group comprises different groups like Black Caribbean groups or people from various indigenous groups in Central America. You may find that individual students or groups or students prefer to be identified as Latinx, whereas others prefer to be identified as their national identity, like *Puertoriqueños* or *Boricuas.* Individuals should identify themselves. It's not our role to identify others on their own behalf nor lump them into labels we create for them out of convenience or lack of taking the time to learn more. In an equity-based school, all students are represented in the language use. If you're not sure how to refer to someone, just ask!

4. Consistently interrupt deficit-thinking and bias about students when interacting with teachers and all staff members. Instead of *That student can't understand any English,* try reframing it as, *That student is developing their English; how amazing to know more than one language! What a process it is to learn another language while also learning content. Whew!* The resources in the leading for equity category on languagelens.com gives more practical advice and examples to ensure that we use and encourage not just asset-based but equity-based language as instructional leaders. Remember, you are a role model in any situation, so always speak as though anyone, including the most vulnerable students and families, are listening. They deserve mutual respect from everyone in the school community.

5. Just as we look at student data to see trends and patterns of disproportionality that may need to be addressed, we also need to look at our staff data as well. Especially important is having *mirrors* for students to see themselves represented in their teachers, leaders, and any staff member at school. Examine your hiring practices to be sure the pool is inclusive and that the job is attractive to all identity groups. Conduct exit interviews to understand if your diversity, equity, and inclusion vision is working and where it can be improved. As instructional leaders, we are social agents who can change the status quo and model inquiry-based, equity-driven changes at all levels. Part of an equity-driven leadership approach is including all subgroups' representatives in major decisions because subgroups are part of the general education population, and their needs should be central. For example, can the MLL Director and Special Education Director be included in all curriculum, instruction, and assessment issues and be part of decisions about policies like student service teams?

CHAPTER 3
LANGUAGE GOALS

THIS CHAPTER FOCUSES ON THE LANGUAGE LENS COMPETENCY OF ACADEMIC language goals: making the invisible visible in our content area.

- ESSENTIAL QUESTION FOR ALL EDUCATORS: How Do We Infuse Language within Our Content Objectives/Goals?
- ESSENTIAL QUESTION FOR COACHES AND LEADERS: How Can Clear Goals Drive Change at the Classroom Level and School Level?

After examining content for academic language aspects, teachers can more effectively plan language goals for all students to reach during any content lesson. Academic language goals help make the nuances of language that can be invisible for language learners more visible and set everyone up for success (Echevarria, Vogt, Short, 2017).).

Failing to plan is planning to fail, as they say. Yet, what if you don't know how to plan for language? That's what we will learn in this chapter. As discussed in the first chapter, starting with the end in mind is key for delivering rigorous, language-rich, and relevant instruction for English learners. To plan effectively for language learners, we must consider who we are teaching and what language is needed to succeed. The last chapter focused on who our learners are and how to integrate their identities into your classroom. This chapter will guide you through how to plan for language goals in your content classroom as you further refine your language lens.

This part of the language lens is when we examine what we are teaching to clarify what language aspects and goals are critical to learning our content area. By examining what academic language students need to succeed, teachers can plan out the *big idea* for a unit or lesson and the corresponding critical academic practices, skills, knowledge, and concepts for both language and content. When we plan lessons, we need to focus less on what activities students need to complete and more on answering these questions clearly: *What do I want students to learn? What do I want students to get out of the lesson?* So that the goals, activities, and impact on students are all aligned (Hattie, 2023).

In this chapter, we will walk through two sets of language-focused planning strategies to keep in mind so you can tighten up your pedagogy. In turn, your English learners' academic language growth can be anticipated, observed, and built upon in future lessons.

The Language Lens Makes the Invisible Visible

A key way to help ensure the acceleration of MLL and ALL performance is to analyze the role of language in your classroom and plan to teach both language and content. You might be thinking, I'm not a trained language teacher. How can I possibly teach all this English language in my classroom? Well, you can! You only need to develop a slightly different lens to look at your units and lessons. This is not about adding more to your plate. This is about seeing what's on your plate differently so that it will be more appetizing or comprehensible for your students. Together, we will uncover ways to plan with language in mind for any content area so that your MLLs, and all your students, can learn the language of your content area, along with the vital knowledge, concepts, and skills. After all, we are all learning language of any content area, so let's ensure we all have the language lens in all classrooms.

Language is all around us. In fact, every content area has its own language to communicate what is important about it—the key skills, the important concepts, and ideas about it. If we already have a strong command of English, we may not see how challenging it can be. By using a language lens to examine what academic language is necessary for our content unit, we can make it more explicit for our students. We can uncover the needed keywords and phrases. We can figure out how we want students to use this vocabulary in sentences and how we want them to put sentences together into paragraphs for specific genres or text types.

We need to develop a language lens through which to plan, teach, and assess academic language. Language cannot be completely separated from the cultural context where it is used. Our classrooms are cultural contexts where learners construct meaning; that is, the relationship between the learner and the learning environment is key in learning for students (Gee, 2008). A lot is going on beneath the surface that language represents, and if we haven't been language learners ourselves, we may not see it or help our students navigate it. Language and culture are intimately connected, and both may be invisible to us if we don't develop our language lens.

Language is ever-changing and influenced by the culture in which it is situated. When the coronavirus pandemic hit, we suddenly started using terms like *social distancing, Zoom fatigue,* and *doomscrolling.* You may not realize it but drag queen culture influences everyday language with terms like: *yaaaas queen, realness, here for it, throwing shade, serving [a look or style].* This subculture, historically marginalized even within the LGBTQ+ community, builds its own terminology and symbols to support its identity (Temko, 2019). Another example of how everyday language is influenced by culture is the immense number of terms that have come and continue to come from African American English (AAE), the historically rich language used in African American communities (Bellamy, 2022). Here are some examples of words and phrases from AAE: *cool, hip, bourgie, slay, tea, totes, peeps, 100%, bae, da bomb, my bad.* Plus, each generation has its own slang. Language changes with the times, man!

The increasing speed of technology via social media simply accelerates how language is shared and how language evolves. Our students are very *hip* to pop culture and its language! Leverage the power of the dynamic cultural landscape that exists outside the school within your classroom. Explicitly teach what *academic language* is, and how it is expected in different contexts while reinforcing that other languages, including social language forms and other dialects, are also valid and valuable forms of communication!

Not only does our language lens help us predict what challenges students may have, but it can also aid us in discovering opportunities to provide appropriate support. Here, we will analyze the aspects that make language challenging in general and in our specific content areas, whether we teach biology, physical education, physics, kindergarten, or guidance. Let's take, for example, a situation that most of us may be able to relate to—getting coffee at a coffee shop.

A Real Life Example

If you've ever been to a fancy café, you know that it has its own culture and language. It has its own cultural context. If you go to this type of establishment regularly, you may feel at ease following the process of ordering your drink of choice. In fact, you may have your order memorized, like, *I'll have a venti decaf caramel macchiato, two pumps vanilla, light drizz.* If that sounds like you, you clearly know what you're doing! Others either have never gone to this type of coffee shop or avoid going because it may be anxiety-provoking. Does this describe you? It makes me so nervous! I'm afraid I'm going to mess up and look stupid trying to order a *regular* cup of coffee! Are you a beginner, intermediate, or advanced learner in this type of situation? Wherever you are on the coffee continuum, let's consider what's at play in terms of language and culture.

When you walk into a fancy coffee shop, you may notice that it differs from your average corner diner. We see in a fancy café that the lighting is usually soft, artwork is displayed, and music is playing. People are there to work quietly, to gather with colleagues or friends, and, of course, to drink various kinds of coffee drinks. However, this coffee experience is more than grabbing your average *cup of joe* at the corner diner. The employees behind the counter of a fancy coffee shop are called *baristas,* and your choices are not *small, medium,* or *large* but instead: *short, tall, grandé,* or perhaps *venti.* There are seemingly endless choices of types of coffee drinks in this kind of place—espresso, macchiato, americano, several kinds of lattes, something iced, and up to seven kinds of iced tea options. The tone of the situation is more formal than informal, with the barista asking, *What can I get started for you?* And the seemingly simple task of getting a cup of coffee can be more complex than one could imagine if you're not proficient in it.

Let's take a *caramel macchiato,* for example, at a Starbucks. If you were to read the definition of a caramel macchiato on the Starbucks website, you would see this:

> The delicious, multi-layered Macchiato begins with milk steamed until it's stretched and smooth to bring out its natural sweetness and is topped by a dense, creamy foam. Then rich espresso is poured over and through the foam, where it mixes with the milk and creates a brown mark on top. Finally, the barista signs their work of art with a crosshatch of sweet caramel sauce. (Starbucks, 2018)

There is no mention of the word *coffee* here at all among three complex sentences. There is figurative language (*work of art*) and technical vocabulary (*barista, stretched milk, crosshatch*). Imagine if this were a text in a class and you were the learner! What would you need to comprehend it? For starters, a visual of what this drink is may help, and a friend to discuss this with beforehand may help scaffold your learning. Consider what else you may need to be successful, and you are putting yourself in your students' shoes as much as possible in terms of thinking about the role of language and culture. Through this exercise, you are further developing your language lens.

Like a Fish out of Water

When unpacking the cultural context of a fancy café, we can reveal these kinds of intricacies of hidden cues and rules, as well as the specific language demands. Since language and culture are so intimately connected, we can't teach one without the other. We now can see that this kind of café can be a metaphor for school for many of our students. If they aren't from that culture, don't have experience with that culture or don't have a comfortable command of the language needed to succeed in that context, they may feel like a *fish out of water*. Likewise, if we are from that culture and language, we may take that water for granted if we don't consider the complexities at play. By taking some time to analyze the demands of language, we can better support our students' experience with it.

Speaking of a fish out of water, one of the biggest demands in English is the spelling system. One may think that each letter in the word fish represents the sound it would typically make—F-I-S-H.

- gh = the f sound like in rouGH
- o = the i sound like in wOmen
- ti = the sh sound like in naTIon

Yet, if we take the separate sounds of F-I-S-H and find them in other English words, we will see that what you see is not what you always get (Beard, 2018)! The word fish, using sounds each letter makes in other English words, comprises the word GHOTI (Essberger, 2018).

English is not a language that is consistent phonetically (whereas languages like Spanish and script systems like Cyrillic are). When we think about the challenges of spelling, never mind the other issues we will discuss later, it's no wonder English can be so tough. Thus, I caution against a *sink-or-swim* model for our multilingual learners—they need the language lens from content teachers to facilitate their English language development, not just content presented without interacting with the language of that content. Again, it's not enough for just the language specialist to support language. While that instructional time matters because the language specialist has the expertise to support English language development specifically, language happens throughout the entire school day!

Now that we've explored a little about the role of culture and the hidden demands of language in different cultural contexts, let's get into how we plan with a language lens.

. . .

The Language Students Need to Be Successful with Content

Once you own the fact that you are, in fact, a teacher of language within the content area(s) you teach, you are ready to plan language goals. When planning a unit of study, it's key to get clear about what language students will need to succeed in your content area, your unit, and each lesson. Students benefit from us being clear about what kind of language they are expected to understand and use during any given lesson so that they can learn the language of our content area.

Remember I said that all teachers are language teachers? Well, it's true. Every content area has language that it uses to communicate its skills, concepts, and ideas! Every subject area in school has its own language—its own phrases, kinds of sentences, and genres/text types. For example, let's consider a ninth-grade algebra classroom. You can see the key words needed to be successful in this content area—*change, effect, up, down, decrease, increase, constant, x-intercept, y-intercept,* and *coordinate plane,* to name a few. Wow, look at all this academic language! Much of the targeted, content-specific vocabulary is evident within our instructional materials—in this algebra classroom, I'm speaking of words like *y-intercept* and *coordinate plan.* However, what about the words and phrases that may not be algebra-specific, like *decrease, increase, change,* and *effect*? Aren't these important too? How do we make sure our students know this vocabulary too. This brings us to *tiered vocabulary.*

Tiered Vocabulary

As mentioned above with the algebra example, vocabulary is important. Students learn new words to help them learn new content. Please keep in mind here that there are different kinds of vocabulary. When I say vocabulary, I am speaking of not just words but also key phrases, or words that go together, needed to succeed in any given unit or content area. One helpful way to think about and plan vocabulary is to look at tiered vocabulary (Tyson, 2013). Tier 1 is comprised of common everyday language. Tier 2 is made up of the words we use across content areas that are more specific than tier 1 words. And tier 3 words are much more technical to a discipline. To exemplify tiered vocabulary, let's look at the language needed to succeed in a sewing class where students are working with patterns (to see the actual student-created, interactive word wall from this sewing class, go to languagelens.com and find the resources on curriculum and instruction):

- Tier 1: *cut, measure, scissors, pins, clean up*
- Tier 2: *shears, stitching, sewing, needle, material, fabric, thread*
- Tier 3: *dressmaker shears, pinking shears, trimming scissors, seam ripper, bobbin, basting stitch, topstitch, zigzag,* plus all the machine parts

I recommend you spend some time with a unit of study to determine what key words and phrases would fall into these tiers. Consider not just tier 3, which seems to get all the attention already in content classrooms, but also those general academic words and everyday words that may not be automatic or obvious for your MLLs. These kinds of words and phrases can actually be the trickiest if we don't make them explicit. Just look at the phrase *clean up*; to *clean up* is different from simply clean. It's not just about knowing verbs in English but the prepositions that, along with verbs, impact their meaning, something known as *phrasal verbs*. Other examples are *get out, get away with, get over, get through, etc.* You may want to simply look online for a sampling of the thousands of phrasal verbs that exist in English and may not be comprehensible to language learners and, thus, may not be *on our radar* as we are planning for students to use language successfully.

Another kind of confusing vocabulary is multiple-meaning words, or homonyms. Let's take the word *needle* featured in the earlier sewing example. A *needle* can mean many things depending on context—something you use for sewing, playing a record, or injecting medication or drugs. In its verb form, to needle means to prod someone. What's more, a not-so-common idiom or expression *is to give someone the needle,* or *needle someone,* meaning that one is heckling or teasing someone. When used in context with others, we can see the challenge of multiple-meaning words more visibly, such as, "Let's *table* our discussion about the periodic *table* until we are all sitting at the *table*." How confusing! These kinds of vocabulary issues are often invisible to native speakers, but they can easily throw an MLL and even an ALL for the proverbial loop! Confusion sets in for many reasons, which is why we don't want to *water down content* but amplify it. An easy way to do this as you work on planning with a language lens is to connect all four domains of language. If you speak something important you want your students to learn, connect it to the written language. Otherwise, only one domain is being utilized, and language is hanging in space without the printed word to ground it. See Figure 3.1 for how the domains of language and literacy are connected. Students make sense of input and output by connecting all four domains. More on this in Chapter 4!

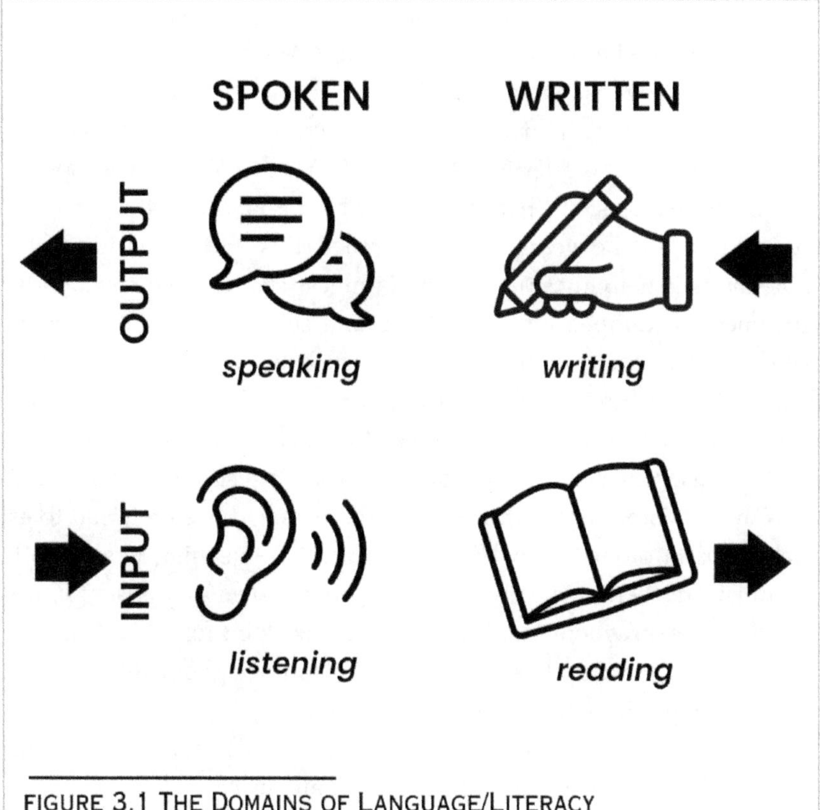

FIGURE 3.1 THE DOMAINS OF LANGUAGE/LITERACY

Figuratively Speaking . . .

Speaking of *giving someone the needle,* let's consider for a moment idioms. Idioms are expressions with literal and figurative meanings, for example, *Don't beat around the bush, It's raining cats and dogs, Luck of the draw, Hold your horses, Go down a rabbit hole,* or *Let's put on our thinking caps.* Again, both ALLs and MLLs can be thrown off by these culturally loaded idioms and other kinds of figurative language (metaphors, similes, hyperbole, symbolism, personification) if we don't use our language lens to point out what they mean.

I will never forget my first IEP meeting as an MLL specialist with an Arabic-speaking family. They declined having an interpreter there because the parents had a strong command of English. However, when the psychologist began the meeting with, "Welcome! The purpose of our meeting today is to *put all of our ducks in a row,*" the parents looked at me questioningly, as if to say, *Ms. Ottow, why are we talking about ducks?* It was a good question. *To put ducks in a row,* figuratively speaking, is an expression that means to be organized, efficient, and prepared. Over the years, I've researched this and other idiomatic expressions to help my students and families. The research never ends! This one has stumped me since I've found several possibilities for its origin. First, it could be from the fact that baby ducks follow behind their mother in a row or fly neatly in a row or V in the sky. Another possibility is when one lines up ducks to shoot in a carnival game. Yet another reason this expression could exist in English vernacular could be from the history of bowling, where the pins had been referred to as ducks, and in order to bowl (*bowl* is a multiple-meaning word, too!), one must put them in a row or series of rows. *Any way you slice it,* it's not a literal expression and, thus, a confusing point for those learning the language. For fun, I've sprinkled idioms throughout this book to see if you notice how commonly we use them!

We use a lot of figurative language in English vernacular, and our language learners need to learn it to operate successfully within the dominant U.S. schooling culture. This means we need to be clear about when we use idioms in our teaching and what support we provide to explain what those expressions mean. We can also tap into students' funds of knowledge by encouraging them to share idioms from their own language!

Keep in mind that idioms may or may not translate across languages. For example, when I lived in Puerto Rico, I learned that the English expression better half can be referred to as your media *naranja,* or your *half orange. ¡Qué romántico!* When I was consulting in Tashkent, Uzbekistan, educators taught me that the English expression *when pigs fly* translates to *when a camel's tail touches the ground* in Uzbek and *when a lobster whistles in the mountain* in Russian. Same meaning with very different ways of expressing it! So don't assume multilingual members of your community don't have idioms or simply figures of speech. in their own language(s).

Let's look at the figure of speech in English, "Mind your own business" or "MYOB." Different linguistic groups across the world express keeping to oneself and not meddling in others' affairs (@DrBlackDeer, 2022):

- *Hai piu pila dell'shecu Prestipino.*/You're fussy and create more issues than the Prestipino's donkey has hair. --Sicilian
- *Mete-te na tua vida.*/ Insert yourself in your own life. --Portuguese
- নিজের চরকায় তেল দাও./Oil your own machine. --Bangla
- *Tu no tienes vela en este entierro.*/ You don't have a candle at this burial. --Puerto Rican Spanish
- Pilipili usiyoila inakuwashia ni?/ Pepper that you didn't eat, why is it burning you? --Swahili
- *Occupe-toi de tes oignons.*/Deal with your own onions. --French
- *Das ist nicht dein Bier.*/That's not your beer. --German
- *Nie mój cyrk, nie moje małpy.*/Not my circus, not my monkeys. --Polish

Comparing and contrasting these cultural aspects of language with staff and students can be fun. If you notice you have idioms as part of your unit of study, or if they come up *on the fly,* you can encourage students to identify them and unpack their literal and figurative meanings. I had a system for students identifying idioms when I taught both in the classroom and also when I was a language specialist and reading interventionist; once we learned about them and made books about their figurative and literal meanings, many felt confident identifying them when we used them in class, shouting out, *Idiom!* to *bring them to light* (see, idioms are everywhere!)

Especially common are idioms from sports and also from the military. Let's look at some military references I often hear in schools: *on the front lines, in the trenches boots on the ground, there's no silver bullet, bullet points, take your best shot, don't shoot yourself in the foot, moving target, shot in the dark, take out the big guns, loose cannon, rally the troops, on your radar, deploy, blow up in your face, rally the troops, shoot from the hip, bite the bullet, jump the gun,* and *pick your battles.* Are we doing battle? No, we are teaching students. However, our lexicon may represent otherwise, even if we just mean it figuratively! Something to think about...

A Language-Rich Content Classroom

Once you know your target words and phrases, think about how you will point these out and post them for students to see and interact with. Posting them on the wall is a starting point, but being sure that students actually use them is important as well. Think about how you will introduce the vocabulary and how students will practice it in different ways and not just by looking up words in glossaries or dictionaries, which has been proven ineffective, as we discuss more in Chapter 5. Students need to use words in context and many times to commit to long-term memory. Instead of just using the dictionary to define words, you can engage students in quick word study and root word analysis activities, interactive word walls, and student-generated academic language notebooks. We want all content classrooms to be language-rich spaces where students read, write, listen, and speak the language they need to succeed.

Academic Language Is More than Just Vocabulary

When planning your language goals and what language we need to teach, we must go beyond vocabulary. Yes, as we just discovered, there are many ways that vocabulary alone can be loaded with potential areas of confusion for our MLLs. However, language is more than key words and phrases. Language also includes how we want students to put vocabulary together into sentences and paragraphs. We shouldn't forget to incorporate this academic language as well when planning for our MLLs and our ALLs. Language can be organized into three levels (Bailey & Huang, 2011; Halliday & Hasan, 1989):

- Words/phrases: vocabulary
- Sentences: language forms

- Discourse: linguistic complexity

Students bring in their knowledge of how words are put into sentences from their home language and, in English, the ways words are put together into sentences, and the syntax (the way words are arranged in a sentence to make meaning) may differ language to language. Therefore, we need to teach sentences explicitly and not assume that students can just *acquire* how English grammar works. As I explained when featured as an expert in Ellevation's Strategies, I explained, "My advice is to start with…the end product, in terms of what language we want our students to produce, whether it be speaking or writing. I always say, *Start with the end in mind; w*hat is the exemplar/product? (Ottow, 20222)" Clearly articulating what success looks like, also called, *success criteria,* is so important, and it's not just the vocabulary! It's how we use language to make meaning. I urge educators to always go back to the content standard and unpack what it asks students to do. Then, with the task in mind, write out the exact target language that students would need to succeed—both for speaking and writing. You don't want it to be a mystery of what you want students to be able to both *understand* and *produce*. Make that academic language crystal clear in your mind and make it visible to your students. Even better is using exemplars and/or mentor text from the discipline you teach so students can see real-world usage of this target language in context.

For example, in the algebra example classroom I mentioned earlier, the teacher is expecting students to speak and write like mathematicians who can *explain* their computation:

> *I know_____ because_____, I agree with _____because _____,* and, *The relation is a function because_______.*

The teacher has provided this target language for the students in the form of *sentence frames* and a word bank with the target vocabulary across all three tiers. These helpful fill-in-the-blank phrases are called sentence frames, sentence stems, or sentence starters, and they give students a jumping off point. The frames provide a clear idea of how to put the vocabulary together to not just form sentences but actually express ideas about the content of this algebra unit of study. Expressing meaning is the whole idea of using language! Plus, math is much more than numeracy; it shows how you know. Language is the vehicle to do that. Just imagine for a moment what kind of conversations may be happening in this classroom about math! Because students know the language expectations for using the words and phrases, they can more easily build on key words and phrases to understand and produce more language in sentences and perhaps even paragraphs. A word of caution, however, about sentence frames: Don't limit students' language to the frames. Our goal is to provide examples through these scaffolds, not limit students' original text/speech or creativity!

Make It Functional!

When you use your language lens to clarify vocabulary and how you expect students to use it in sentences and paragraphs, you can bring that academic language to the surface and make it visible and explicit for your students. You can see that although vocabulary is extremely important, it's not all there is to language. We need to go a little deeper into how the language is used in terms of sentences and discourses in our content area.

When planning language goals, it can be beneficial to think about the language function you expect and make that language explicit. What is the language asking students to do? *Explain? Compare/contrast? Describe? Justify?* As a content teacher, it's essential to use your language lens to find the function of what the language is doing with the discipline-specific topics of your content area. You are, in fact, having students read what scientists wrote if you're teaching science, or teaching students how to prepare and respond to work orders if you're teaching autobody mechanics in a tech school, or equipping students to write a narrative if you teach Language Arts. Whatever we teach, they are *functions* of the language we expect students to interact with—reading, writing, listening, and speaking. Make the *function of the target language* more visible. See Figure 3.2 for a helpful formula for language goals or language objectives. I find that you need to find your own formula based on your style and, of course, the task in your content area. Take a look at my examples and adjust as you see fit.

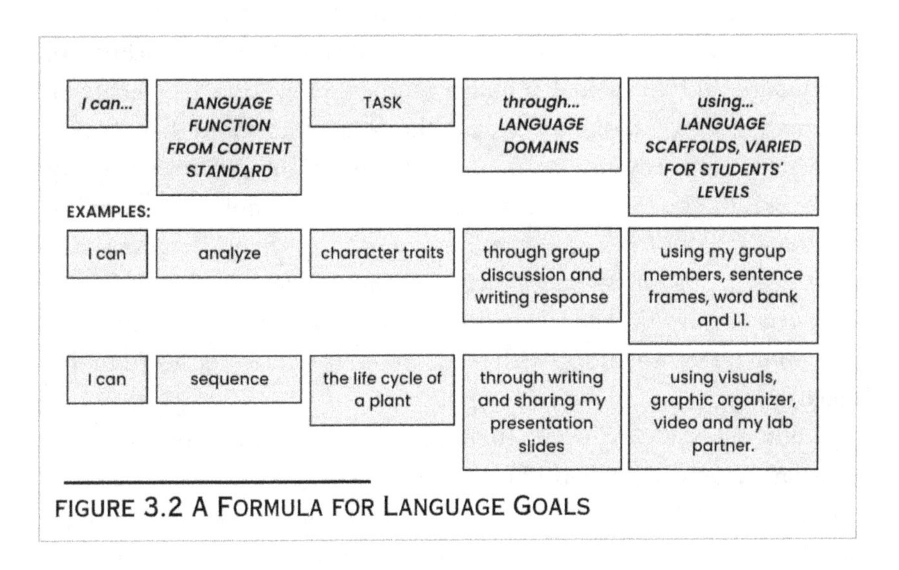

FIGURE 3.2 A FORMULA FOR LANGUAGE GOALS

Analyze the Demands of the Academic Language

To make the language we expect students to use to be successful in any content area more visible, we need to analyze what the language is demanding of our students. When teaching language through a functional perspective, students can see the demands of language, and language itself can become a vehicle for learning instead of being a barrier (Dutro & Kinsella, 2010). One way to think about using academic language purposefully is what function we are using it for (Halliday & Matthiessen, 1961). For example, in math class, the students use evidence to support claims about their algebra problems. They are expected to agree or disagree, which is essentially the language function of arguing, persuading, or giving opinions.

Other examples of language functions include *paraphrasing, elaborating, inferring, synthesizing, discussing,* and *informing*. Some educator teams I work with who use the understanding by design (UBD) framework (McTighe & Wiggins, 2012) also think about language functions as the transfer skills that cross disciplines. For example, persuasion and supporting claims with evidence are both important skills that students should be able to do in any content area. (I've also used the concept of *Essential Questions* from UBD to ground each chapter, as you may have noticed.) In 2000, Averil Coxhead from the School of Linguistics and Applied Language Studies at Victoria University of Wellington, New Zealand, created the Academic Word List (AWL) from 570 word families used across twenty-eight different areas of study, so if you know the word *construct*, it's not a far leap to *constructed, constructing, construction, constructions, constructive, constructs, reconstructs, reconstructed, reconstructing, reconstruction* and *reconstructs.* I've included Dr. Coxhead's website in the Bibliography for you to reference (along with many other useful references from this book!).

Knowing how you want students to function with your key academic language will be helpful for you in planning a precise sequence of lessons but most importantly for your students so they know the target and when they get there! Go to langaugelens.com to get Confianza's Language Functions Tool. Figure 3.2 gives a sneak peek. This will show you what you can make visible right away using key words, sentence structures, and graphic supports for cross-curricular language functions.

LANGUAGE FUNCTION	GRAPHIC ORGANIZER	BEGINNER Q & A STEMS	INTERMEDIATE Q & A STEMS	ADVANCED Q & A STEMS
ELABORATE/ EXPLAIN KEY WORDS: because of, clearly, due to, evidence, for this reason, furthermore, moreover	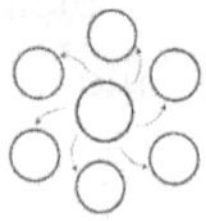	Can you tell me more about...? What do you think about...?	What makes you think...and why? Why did you say/write...?	Have you also considered...? How did you come to that?
		I think... I believe...	I think...because... I think it means that...	In other words... Going off ...'s point, ... Due to...

FIGURE 3.2 A SNEAK PEEK AT CONFIANZA'S LANGUAGE FUNCTIONS TOOL

One final word about language goals is to think about genres and text types when you expect students to write, speak, read, and/or listen to multiple sentences or paragraphs. For instance, are they expected to comprehend and/or produce narrative, procedural, or expository text? Are they retelling or discussing? Consider what text types or genres you use in your classroom. Look at how the author organizes text to reveal what language structures you probably expect from your students but may not have made fully clear to them. Providing and teaching with graphic organizers matched to text structure, especially when it comes to showing models, or mentor texts, of discipline-specific literacy where we close read *with* students (e.g., how scientists write, how mathematicians write), is a high-leverage strategy I promote to all teachers who are expecting students to use language to understand or express in a genre. To be clear, when I refer to texts, I am including a multiliteracies approaching, including visual, oral, musical and kinesthetic texts, too.

If we take the sewing class example we discussed earlier, we can imagine the students writing or talking through how to make a pattern, which would be a procedural language. The language goal here could be I can sequence how to make a zippered bag using sequencing words. Better yet, walking students through an example of what you're looking for in the form of a student exemplar or a mentor text in the form of the written instructions that come with a sewing pattern could really go a long way. Having clear language goals around sequencing words like *first, next, then,* and *last* and a graphic organizer showing steps in order would likely support students in the content and language of sewing or putting any procedure in a logical order.

Planning Language Goals

We have discussed the pieces of academic language, including the part of vocabulary, sentences, genres, and text types to make visible in your planning. It may now sound like common sense to set clear language and content goals, but *common sense isn't always so common*! Remember that many educators are learning how to teach academic language, so you are not alone. Here are some tips for planning clear language goals:

1. Review an upcoming unit of study and make a list of key words and phrases at tiers 1–3, not just tier 3! Think about what general academic (tier 2) and everyday (tier 1) language might be really challenging for language learners. Include phrasal verbs, multiple-meaning words, and idioms.
2. *Speak of the devil!* Idioms! With your team or your students, see how many idioms you hear or read in a single day or class period. You could invite multilingual students to share versions from their own or encourage them to look them up or ask their families about them. You could see just how many sports-related idioms you all can think of and then analyze them to compare the literal meaning to the figurative one! Once you hear and see idioms, you can't go back. Equip students and your colleagues with this critical part of the language lens.
3. Imagine how you want students to use the vocabulary and write out the *exact sentences* you'd like for them to be able to both understand and produce. Writing out your expectations for language use will help you clarify the success criteria for your tasks. Consider what language functions you expect from all students as they learn the content.
4. Use the success criteria you developed in #3 above to then backward plan the sentence frames and even paragraph frames. Don't just create language frames out of nowhere! Use the target language function and language structures you want all students to be proficient with. If you have examples from other classrooms or students from classes in the past, use those to refer to. Plus, look at the texts from your discipline as models (e.g., a news video that *explains,* a letter to the editor that *persuades,* etc.)
5. Consider the genre / text type students will be reading and / or writing. Plan for the support of a graphic organizer to exemplify the structure of the genre. If you expect

students to write this text type, provide exemplars or mentor texts from your content area. I can't stress *modeling* the language enough!

6. Consider the power of starting your goals with "I can" versus the non-student-centered SWBAT (students will be able to). Make sure this is for the students, not just for you!
7. The important thing here is to make the invisible aspects of language more visible and to do so in a way that works for you and, most importantly, your students. In our content instruction, students' language proficiency can be accelerated when we explicitly teach these aspects or features (Echevarria, Short, & Powers, 2006; Snow & Uccelli, 2009). Some of you may have shared expectations for both content and language goals already in place in your school, grade level, or department. I recommend making that work for you so the goals are student-friendly and guide for students to know if they've hit the mark. If you don't already have something like this in place, try it out! And if you're lucky enough to have a language specialist to consult, don't hesitate to do so. I've found many ways of writing language objectives and goals, not necessarily one "right" way. Mix and match different formulas to see what works. We've focused here a lot on the unit level, so you can start at this high level, but you can certainly do that for your lessons as well. Lesson-level goals for language are often referred to as language objectives. Whether you decide to try or refine language goals for units and/or lessons, as I said earlier, please be intentional about how these are useful for students so that they can be successful with the key language aspects you know they need to be successful in your content instruction.

~

TIPS FOR TEACHERS: HOW DO WE INFUSE LANGUAGE WITHIN OUR CONTENT OBJECTIVES/GOALS?

1. What language can you make explicit for your students, including tiered vocabulary and key language functions for each lesson and/or unit? Is the purpose of using the key language of your content area clear so that students are not just focused on language but they also know what they are supposed to do with the language (i.e., *analyze, identify, elaborate*)? Refer to Confianza's Language Functions Tool at languagelens.com for more ideas.

2. Are you inadvertently using challenging and cultural figurative language (e.g., saying, *Time is money,* when asking students to hurry up; using the symbol of the Roman goddess Justitia when discussing the American justice system) that may not be clear to students? If so, how can you be sure your students understand what this kind of figurative language means? Can you invite in small teachable moments to do so? Can you allow students to share their perspectives on linguistically tricky words and phrases to boost metacognition and metalinguistic awareness?

3. Are there ways you can collaborate with your content team members, your language specialist, and/or a coach to plan more intentionally for language in your content area? Here are some ideas to do on your own or with a team:

4. Review your curriculum for tiered vocabulary. The technical words, or tier 3 words, are often presented for us in the form of lists and boldface throughout published instructional materials. However, remember that the curriculum is more than the published materials! We can and should often enhance the texts and other published resources to meet the needs of our students since they don't always

come that way. Analyze if there are other tier 3 words or phrases that your students might need. Then use your language lens to do the same for tier 2 and tier 1 words and phrases.

5. Consider what language tools, or scaffolds, you currently have available for students to meet the academic language goals and what could be created or added to make the language of your content area more accessible (more ideas in Chapter 5). See if these language tools can be made more explicit for students across classrooms so they can see that to analyze is to analyze, no matter what content area they are in, for example. By strengthening the system with a language lens, we create more cohesion for students who can spend much of their day jumping between content areas and even between teachers.

6. Provide exemplars of what the target language should look like and sound like. Be clear that specific disciplines and genres have specific kinds of language, often referred to as disciplinary literacy. If you teach science, for example, "This is how scientists write. Let's look at an actual scientific report to learn about the language of a scientist." Point out key language features like sentence structures and key words used in continuous text to make the language more visible for your MLLs and ALLs (e.g., *as a result; therefore*).

7. Show how the text and speech in your discipline can also be structured through graphic organizers and keep graphic tools available when students are both reading and writing. For example, in a science report, the structure or language function could be *sequencing* steps in a cycle. Use a simple arrow graphic organizer to show how the function of this language occurs and what specific language to use when learning about or processing steps in a process. For all these tips, check out the resources for curriculum and instruction with a language lens at languagelens.com.

~

TIPS FOR COACHES AND LEADERS: HOW CAN CLEAR GOALS DRIVE CHANGE AT THE CLASSROOM LEVEL AND SCHOOL LEVEL?

1. One major takeaway I hope each of you can get from this guidebook is that we need to be aware of and integrate what I referred to in Chapter 1 as *parallel practices* between what we expect at the classroom level and what we expect at the adult learning level. It isn't enough to expect teachers to engage students in meaningful ways if we aren't engaging staff just as meaningfully. We need to *practice what we preach* (Idiom!) The last thing teachers need is to sit through a workshop or PLC that is *not* modeling the very strategies asking them to use with students! In the first chapter, I encouraged you to list your look-fors in the classroom. You asked yourself, *What does equitable instruction look like? Sound like? Feel like?* Now, please do the same thing but for staff development and the professional learning culture in your school. I don't just mean formal spaces like workshops or common planning time. I mean ALL spaces, ALL parts of your school culture. How do you want your school to include all learners and clarify expectations for all staff? What's working? What could be improved going forward?

2. Whether you are a coach or a leader, examine the goals of your school. Do you have a focused goal or set of goals? Do the goals make sense and connect to each other? Or does your school suffer from *initiative overload*? Make sure staff can share their perception of what expectations you have for them. Even if you, as an instructional leader, can *see the forest for the trees* of how your multiple school goals are important and connected to each other, it doesn't mean everyone you support can see that same vision and strategy. Consider revising your school goals so that it is focused and that everyone can see we are moving in the same direction, together.

. . .

3. Next, once the school goals are clear, align educator goals to that larger, shared goal and support everyone moving towards that goal. If your school requires professional practice goals and student learning goals, for example, do a deep dive with your team to see if the goals could connect better to the school goal. For example, if a school sees that student data shows a need to improve writing and vocabulary development, then let's guide educators to all work on that in their goals. We can plan a professional learning map for the year that is focused and aligned on writing and vocabulary across the content areas, not a hodgepodge of one-off workshops or events that may not help us work smarter together. For more on this, see the resources on data and assessment at languagelens.com.

4. If you are a supervisor, reflect on your evaluation process. Are you accurately placing teachers on a continuum of teacher development scores based on evidence in the classroom? Or are you inflating their scores (or deflating their scores) for some reason? Work with other leaders to calibrate what *proficient* is. Go back to your look-fors that we discussed in Chapter 1 and other tools for evaluation and coaching to be sure that teachers have these in place. Use student data to support teacher evaluation, including teacher goals which we will discuss in the next chapter.

5. In your learning walk process, if you don't already have a basic protocol for asking students what they are learning and why, please implement it now. *What are you learning? Why are you learning it? Do you understand what you are learning? How do you know? What do you like about it? What don't you like about it?* Probing students, in my opinion, is one of the most effective ways we can get an accurate view of what is working or not working in classrooms. See the resources for leading for equity at languagelens.com for more guidance in this area.

CHAPTER 4
READING, WRITING, LISTENING, AND SPEAKING IN EVERY CLASSROOM

THIS CHAPTER FOCUSES ON THE LANGUAGE LENS COMPETENCY OF THE domains of language: reading, writing, listening, and speaking in every lesson.

- ESSENTIAL QUESTION FOR ALL EDUCATORS, ESPECIALLY TEACHERS: How Do We Ensure Language-Rich Learning Spaces for All Learners?
- ESSENTIAL QUESTION FOR COACHES/LEADERS: How Do We Support Educators in their Development of Inclusive, Engaging, Language-Rich Classrooms?

All students benefit from engaging across all language domains in every lesson—reading, writing, listening, and speaking—so that both literacy and oral language are parts of content instruction for deeper learning and longer-term use of new content and language. Throughout this chapter, I will practically be begging you, educators, to please go beyond what I like to call *random acts of discourse*. Plan for student interaction and *equity of voice* through academic discussions. Center students in the learning and hear them using language meaningfully.

Simply put, the four domains of language are reading, writing, listening, and speaking. We want all these domains happening for all students in every classroom, in every lesson, every day! Sounds like common sense, right? Well, I've said it before, and I'll say it again in this book: *common sense isn't so common,* as it turns out. As content teachers, we may have been neither taught nor conditioned to really think about being sure that reading, writing, listening, and speaking are intentional parts of *all* lessons. We may have been trained to *cover the content,* not necessarily paying heed to how language in the form of these domains can actually help students *learn and process* that content, any content, to be honest. This belief that we teach through stand-and-deliver may have been reinforced by large-scale assessments we need to give that often stress mainly the retention of knowledge and skills over how students actually interact with the content through language.

Covering the Curriculum with Care

Indeed, there are times when we need to get a lot of information across, and students need to listen for longer. Of course. But what I'm saying here is we can refine our language lens by reflecting on how much students use language beyond simply listening. Are they getting time to speak? Are they getting time to read? To write? As discussed in Chapter 1, the shifts of the career- and college-readiness standards stress these shifts—building oral language skills, reading complex texts, and writing across the curriculum. I invite you to take stock of where you are in these shifts by analyzing how you incorporate the language domains in your instruction as you move through this chapter. You may find you're missing tiny yet powerful opportunities for more language development for your students by more effectively incorporating the domains.

With the emphasis on college and career standards, we know that all teachers need to be focused on literacy and oracy in their content classrooms. As I like to say, while college and career are important, let's also focus on students being *life ready*! Students need to have a command of language to express themselves, to be informed citizens, to make choices, and to exercise their rights in society. They need to read, write, listen, and speak confidently and thoughtfully. In my view, students need to be able to *reach for the stars* and pursue their interests, their hopes, and dreams. Language helps get us there. We need to not only teach the curriculum but also know our students, consistently check for understanding, and work collaboratively to meet learning targets. If we can all get behind this goal, then we can all institute more learning experiences that set students up to use language in meaningful ways. So let's begin exploring what this means and how we do it effectively!

The Domains of Language

The four domains of language can be divided into two general channels of input and output. The input channels are comprised of listening and reading. Either by listening or reading, we take in information. These can also be referred to as the receptive domains. The opposite is the output channel. Speaking and writing make up how we express or share information, often referred to as the productive or expressive.

Along with speaking and writing, we could also consider visual arts and nonverbal communication like nods, smiles, and shrugging (although nonverbal cues can vary widely by culture!) to be part of output channels. For our purposes here, we will focus on reading and writing as the input channels and listening and speaking as the output channels because reading, writing, listening, and speaking are imperative to improve our content classrooms. Yet, we can keep in mind that these other modalities of expression are just as valid and should not be ignored as ways to express oneself.

Be aware, though, of body language's role when instructing and formatively assessing students' comprehension of instruction. If a student looks lost or confused, take the time to check-in. Use *thumbs-up/thumbs-down* as a simple comprehension check or a way for students to express that they need help (however, be aware that this signal can be an offensive gesture in some cultures, so be sure its use is clear for your students). As we will review in this chapter, the power of student-to-student interaction can greatly help with the input of instruction and the output through continuous, formative assessment of student output of their learning.

. . .

Links Between Oracy and Literacy

We can look at the input and output channels, but just as important are the links between reading and writing to one another, and listening and speaking to one another. Reading and writing are intimately connected as *literacy* modalities. While listening and speaking are connected as *oral language* modalities. You might be thinking, *I don't teach literacy! I don't teach oral language! I have no training in either, and I have no idea how to do this in my content classroom.* Rest assured, I've worked with hundreds upon hundreds of educators who have said similar things to me, and they have found ways to enhance their teaching through small changes in implementing activities for reading, writing, listening, and speaking. Do your students talk in your classroom? If the answer is yes, you have oracy, or oral language, happening in your classroom. Do students read and write in your classroom? Then, behold, you have literacy in your classroom as well! Paying attention to the little things you do with a language lens going forward can have a huge payoff for your students. As they say, *the small things are the big things*.

When it comes to enacting a language lens that actually makes a difference for students, the small things are indeed the big things. One slight adjustment in engaging across all language domains can go a long way. That's what the language lens is, a different way to see and then act. Incremental change is what we must strive for. Plus, one small adjustment can help a teacher notice the power he or she has over students' learning and, more importantly, as I'll share in this chapter and the next, students' ownership of their learning. I'm often asked by principals and district administrators, *If you could start with one thing to change classroom practice for language learners, what would it be?* My answer is, *Let's first decrease the amount of teacher talk and increase the amount of student talk.*

Teacher Talk versus Student Talk

Typically, an adult brain can listen well for ten to twenty minutes, and with that, on average, we don't necessarily retain all of what we hear (Rehn, 2016)! So imagine what an MLL student goes through. Do we want to sound like Charlie Brown's teacher? If you don't know this cultural reference, this American cartoon series had the teacher in the background of the child characters as an incoherent droning voice: *Wah-wah-wah-wah-wah-wah!*

We may have been schooled by the "sage on the stage" model of lecturing, being the transmitter of information to students who are "empty vessels" to be filled with knowledge. But that is not the way of the now. Not only does this transmission-based model of education doesn't work for all learners, let's face it, it's neither engaging nor does it square with our modern age of interaction and multiple modalities. We know more about learning, we know more about the brain, and we know more about the rich diversity of our students now. We know that we need to be dynamic, interactive, multimodal, and promoting of student ownership of learning to reach and teach our learners!

Think of your own experience as an adult learner. Recall a recent learning experience you had, whether it be a professional development workshop or a conference you attended. What worked for you? What didn't work? Do you appreciate sitting and listening to someone go on and on for an indeterminate amount of time without some kind of interaction? Likely the answer is no. Gone are the days—we hope!— of lecture-based learning being the only way to impart knowledge, particularly in secondary classrooms. Students won't *learn* the language (and content!) if they don't *use* it!

Shifting to More Interactive Ways of Learning

A big part of the twenty-first-century teaching we discuss throughout this book is shifting our paradigm around how students best learn. And for our language learners, the need is vastly clear to make instruction as meaningful and language-rich as possible. And if we make our instruction more MLL-friendly, it is not just good for MLL students but also for ALL students!

How many times have I walked into a classroom where a teacher, with the best of intentions, has students listening passively for the bulk of the class period? In my role as a teacher evaluator and leadership coach, I encourage classroom observations to gather pointed data collection, which, for teachers of MLLs, largely revolves around how much language students are producing and the quality and quantity of language. I determine the ratio between student talk time and teacher talk time. I also observe how actively students are listening, which can range from students actually listening, to students *pretending* they are listening, to students completely disengaged and not afraid to show it! Then I will share that student discourse data with teachers and with leaders, and we will all debrief to see if it was the teacher's intention to have the bulk of the class period be students sitting and listening to the teacher talking versus rich conversation, writing, and reading tasks, instruction that is more active and engaging. It usually is not the intention of the teacher to have that much time spent on listening!

Reflect on Your Ratio

Just as I explained earlier, as a teacher coach or evaluator may do to support increasing purposeful student talk, you, as a teacher, can evaluate—or assess—yourself. You can set a timer during your lesson when you begin speaking and see how many minutes your teaching adds up to. You could bravely record yourself and play it back, simply tallying the number of minutes you're presenting information and the number of minutes students are interacting. This method can also help you hear what kind of instructional language you are using and if it's unintentionally confusing students with untaught idioms—for example, *Put on your thinking caps* or *Let's head out the door.* This is in relation to the often-hidden challenges in idiomatic language, as discussed in the previous chapter.

Types of Student Talk

Now you can break it down even further into two types of student talk. You can examine if you've provided an opportunity where students talk to you, which can take place in whole-group or even during small-group or individualized instruction, perhaps in the form of a conference. Let's refer to this as *student-to-teacher talk*. You can also track opportunities you've provided for students to talk with one another—not just small talk or chatter that is unproductive! I'm talking about purposeful student-to-student interaction that has clear expectations and supports. Discourse—complete thoughts using multiple sentences where students exchange ideas and information—is the goal. This could be in the form of cooperative groups where students have a task at hand with clear roles and language structures to use with one another. Let's call students talking to other students—whether it be in pairs, triads, or other group configurations—*student-to-student talk*.

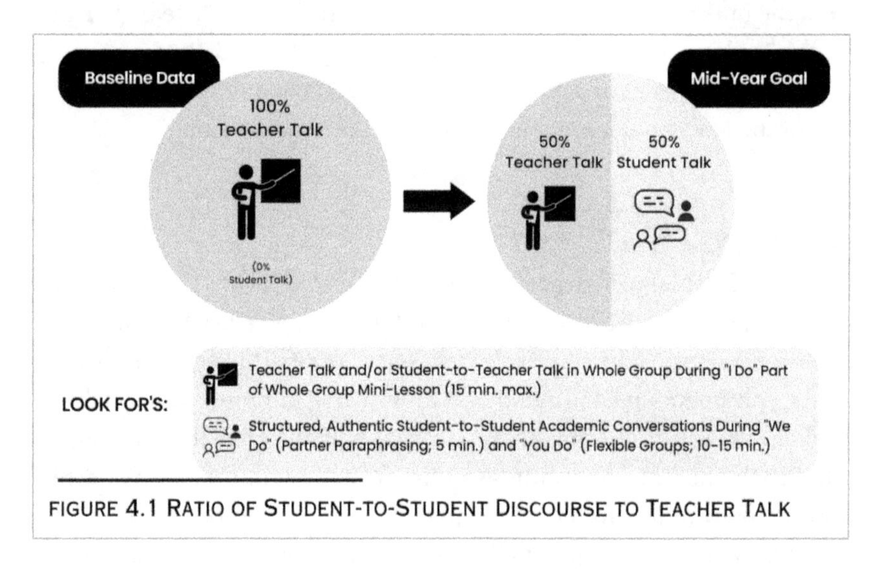

FIGURE 4.1 RATIO OF STUDENT-TO-STUDENT DISCOURSE TO TEACHER TALK

If you look at Figure 4.1, imagine that in this hypothetical classroom, there wasn't any student-to-student talk at play in the pie chart on the left. However, let's envision that this teacher is setting the goal of increasing student discourse in his practice, not just calling on students in whole-group discussion, or ping-ponging. In my consulting work with coaches and leaders, I teach various methods for measuring student discourse in real-time during observations to track this data over time as a coaching and observation tool (go to langaugelens.com for more information and tools). Moreover, I believe that teachers can and should be self-aware of their ratio so that students get *equity of voice*. Who is doing the talking is often who is doing the learning. Often just building in this awareness, teachers realize that their *air time* may be dominating students to actually process what they are learning. Chunk and chew!

No More Ping-Ponging

If you've ever played the game of Ping-Pong, you know that the one ball goes back and forth between the two players (or two-on-two players if you're playing

doubles). Now imagine yourself as the teacher, as a Ping-Pong ball, and your, let's say, twenty-five students are who you're playing in Ping-Pong. Then, if you're only implementing whole-group instruction and students have questions or are answering questions, you are literally ping-ponging in up to twenty-five directions. Now let's contrast this with intentionally breaking up the class into five groups of five students each. Once you've given them a task and clear expectations bolstered by support, then you essentially give the ball over to the students. You now have the role of facilitating learning rather than being the primary conveyer of it. If you're fortunate to co-teach, you can *really* make the most of having two instructors in the room by parallel teaching by splitting the class in half or facilitating multiple groups in a workshop model.

By redesigning the physical structures through which your students learn, you put more power into their hands (see Figure 4.2). Students already come to us with so much power, we just have to harness it! Let's give students more ownership over their learning and, thus, with the appropriate tasks and scaffolds, the opportunity to show what they know by discussing it with their peers. Frequently, students can teach one another better than we can teach them! Peer-to-peer learning cannot be understood in a language-rich classroom. Plus, you're using the economy of time and language more effectively by breaking it up and turning it over to the students. Another benefit of group learning is that students who may not speak up in the whole group may feel comfortable and those needing practice in the target language will get practice in their group as a built-in scaffold before they speak up in a larger group or perhaps write about it. We will look more closely at grouping as a key scaffold for students in the next chapter. But for now, I'd like for you to think about it, if you haven't already, as a key structural change in your classroom that can boost oral language and facilitate deeper learning and, overall, a more student-centered and engaging classroom.

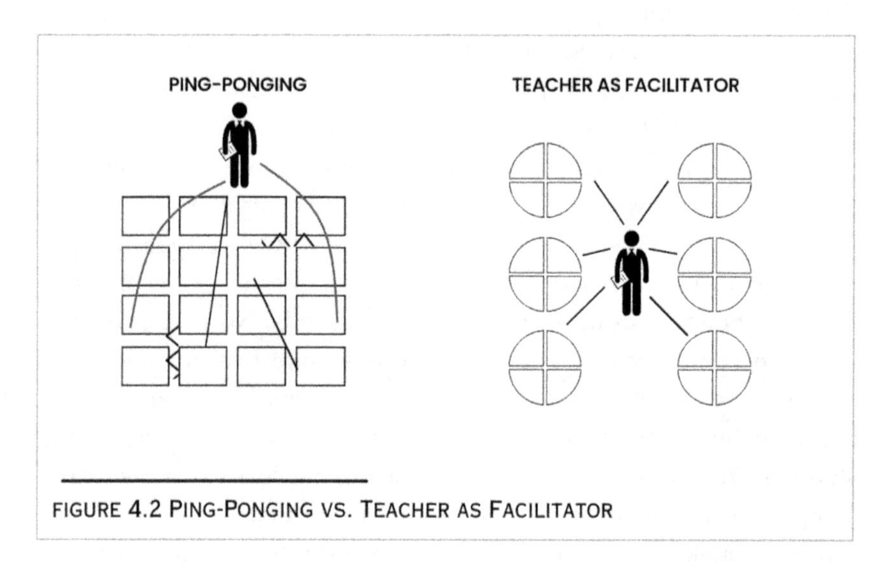

FIGURE 4.2 PING-PONGING VS. TEACHER AS FACILITATOR

Appropriate Expectations

Remember that our MLL students' language development occurs through a long-term process that connects all language domains. For MLLs, their proficiency in their heritage language or languages is also a major factor and one of their greatest resources. Please remember, though, that it all comes back to knowing our students and differentiating for them as best as we can. If we have a newcomer who is not ready to speak and is still in the silent period, we will not force that child to speak. He or she could follow along and input into discussions, when appropriate, through supported activities like matching, listing, or drawing. The amount of language we expect from a student increases with language level. Likewise, the number of scaffolds may decrease as the level increases. I say that the scaffolds may decrease because different learners require different supports to learn. Plus, because language is fluid and varies by context, we need to be aware of this fact, not having a fixed mindset around what our students can or can't do (Gibbons, 2002; Council of Chief State School Officers, 2023).

Boosting Oral Language

As stated, oral language development must be a part of our instruction with MLLs. Students need to practice out loud what they hear to develop across all domains, particularly literacy. Think about it. If you were to go to, say, Romania right now, without knowing Romanian, and listen to people all day long, would you be able to start speaking Romanian proficiently right away? Probably not. Likewise, if you were to begin writing in Romanian as a beginning language learner, wouldn't you also want to *repeatedly hear and practice it through speech*? The answer is YES! (I can relate to this remark because I consulted for an English-speaking school in Romania for years. Each time I went to Bucharest, I tried to use more and more Romanian greetings in my interactions while interacting around the city. It's important for me not to present as an *Ugly American* who refuses to learn any of the host country's language, including simple greetings to show respect. Part of my value system is to honor the language and culture I get to visit, so I start with simple phrases like *Buna zuia/Hello, Please,* and *Thank you. Bună!*)

In order to become more comfortable with a new language and, ultimately, store it in our longer-term memory, we must practice, practice, practice, and we need that practice to occur through both oracy and literacy. One primary strategy for boosting oral language is through intentional academic conversations in peer pairs or groups. Intentionally grouping students is a way to help them process the concepts and skills being taught in a way that goes beyond a simple *turn and talk.* Students learn so much from each other, when we give them the structures to work together effectively and just get out of their way! Ultimately, we want students to love learning and be able to express themselves, going above rote recall to sharing their opinions with each other and building on each other's ideas, for example.

• • •

Academic Conversations

Turn and talk—or simply turning to a partner to review what was just taught—is an effective way to *chunk and chew* content in a language-rich way. I use turn and talk, think-pair-share, and other grouping structures all the time in professional development training with teachers. This is because I want to model why this is so effective with learners of any age. I repeated say to educators, as I did in a recent interview, "It doesn't just happen. Students need to be taught these skills to express their ideas, to really share their opinions. Bottom line, students need to *practice* the language to be proficient at it." (Ottow, 2022, as featured in Ellevation Education, 2022). Students need to go deeper with language to really process and retain the meaning of the complex content of our career- and college-readiness standards. Academic conversations, also known as academically productive talk and accountable talk, have students engaged in active listening and using specific sentence stems to produce content language. It's a way to structure academic discourse through meaningful oral language use. The pandemic's online-only instruction showed me the need for student voice more than ever! How about you?

As I've said before in this book, this guide is meant to survey key practices, or competencies, that help content teachers with a language lens. You can certainly go deeper into any of the ideas presented, and this one is no different. I definitely recommend that you go to languagelens.com to explore resources on academic conversation in the curriculum and instruction category. For a sneak peek, look at Figure 4.3 for a way to structure paraphrasing through a simple yet powerful structured strategy we call *Paraphrasing Partners.*

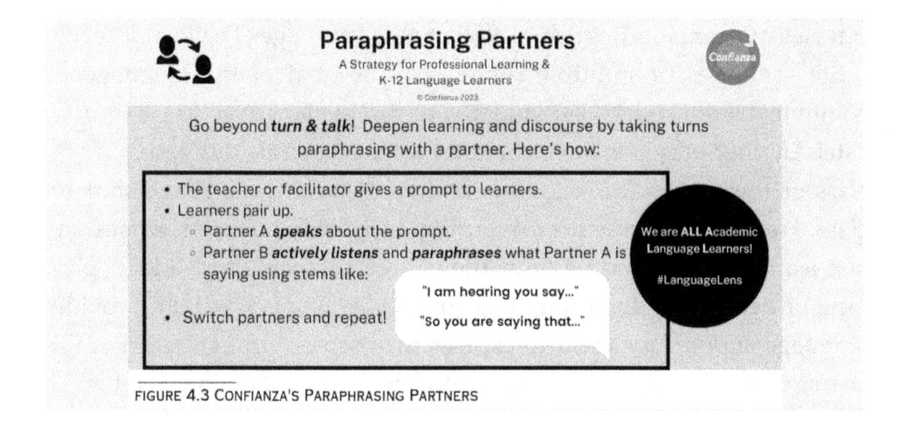

FIGURE 4.3 CONFIANZA'S PARAPHRASING PARTNERS

Writing in Any Classroom

If oral language supports literacy development, how can we further boost literacy? First, we can more intentionally plan moments for students to write every day in every class. It's not just the job of the Language Arts teacher to get students to write. Career- and college-readiness standards promote writing across the curriculum. *Even in physical education class or art class, or cooking class?* You may ask. The answer is *yes.* I have worked with teachers in every subject area at every grade level, and we are getting kids to write, write, write! It's about the conditions we create, remember. If we have the tools available and the expectations set up, students can do amazing things for us! One high-leverage way for students to write daily is to have a quick-write prompt. A quick-write prompt has students writing in a no-pressure, nongraded way every day. Some schools have activities at the beginning of the class period, often called a Do Now or Bell Ringer, where a prompt can be provided for students to respond to, like clockwork, every day. Likewise, an end-of-less exit ticket can be a quickly written, nongraded response that supports language development and doubles as a quick formative assessment for educators to guide students' learning.

I'm a huge fan of visual thinking for quick writing. How do we do this? Teachers post a painting or other image related to the content at hand and have students describe what they see. Students can jot down phrases or words in English or their home language. They could even write sentences or multiple sentences. The goal of the language is communication, so let's get students to use the language to communicate! Another idea is to have students write what they did yesterday in class or their goals for the week. It doesn't have to be at the start of class. We can have students use writing to quickly reflect on what they just learned in the middle or at the end of a lesson. For MLLs beginning or developing their language journey in English, we can provide language support for them to express themselves through writing. I'll share some language scaffolding ideas later in the following chapter.

Close Reading and Annotating Text

Those of us who have been teaching literacy and language for a long time may laugh out loud upon hearing that the strategy of analyzing text through close reading and annotation is now a "mainstream" one. We may laugh out of sheer joy because we've been promoting it for years! I heard one reading specialist comment to me lately, *Close reading? You mean, actually, teaching kids how to read? This is a new standards-based strategy for all classrooms now! Hooray!* Yes, this strategy is a victory for all students—MLLs, students developing literacy, and special education students—and a move forward for all teachers since we are all teachers of language. And part of language is teaching how to read, along with teaching how to write, speak, and listen!

In terms of reading, a strategy that career- and college-readiness standards promote is one called annotating text through close reading, a way to engage with text meaningfully, connecting themes to the students' lives and background knowledge. Close reading through annotating text is simply a way to code text in ways that make sense for the students to signal what's important, what they connect to, and what questions they may have. You may be doing this automatically as you read this book. You may have your own text annotation system—highlighting key passages that resonate with you, folding over pages you want to go back to, adding a question mark or exclamation point to parts you have questions about or that make a big point. See Figure

4.5 for some ideas, many of which you may be using already when reading this book! If you're reading this as an e-book, you may also use the available digital annotations. For more on close reading, go to languagelens.com and check out the resources in the category for curriculum and instruction.

For many, many readers, text annotation can support our close reading of a text. Proficient readers may or may not use annotation, but they are all *reading closely* through the automaticity they have developed when learning to read. We want to make this process visible, both metacognitively and metalinguisticly, for our students so they can see how to get there. I find that many secondary students read well below grade level, yet their needs (both MLL and ALL) are not met when it comes to scaffolding grade-level text. Well, let's remember that any teacher can implement close reading through text annotation to help students connect to the text and access grade-level content. Any teacher can model how to read a text deeply by thinking aloud as they read and bringing students into that process by having each student annotate what the teacher is projecting. Model, model, model!

Pre-Reading

Another key point about reading is to spend time thinking about, talking about, and writing about the text before actually reading it. Setting a purpose for reading (or viewing a video, for example!) and engaging with the topic beforehand is called *pre-reading*. Here are some simple and effective pre-reading strategies: thinking aloud by predicting what the text will be about, doing a picture walk or text feature tour, do the K and W in a KWL chart (*What do you KNOW about the topic? What do you WANT to know?*) or intentional discussion before reading it. Analyzing text features (headings, captions, diagrams, illustrations) and predicting what we think the text will be about before we read it can go a long way in terms of providing students access to content. I'm a big fan of the *stop-and-jot* strategy before, during, and after reading with adults or K-12 students. For example, *stop and jot one phrase or sentence about what you just read in your own words*, or *write down a word summarizing what we have learned so far and* (bonus!) *share it with your partner.*

Additionally, if we provide time and structures for students to discuss what they see in the text features and what connections they can make to prior knowledge as well as ask questions, we can *hook* them into reading versus just saying, *Turn to page 45 and read to yourself so you can answer the questions on page 49.* How is that motivating? I ask. How is that teaching? Students need to interact with text and with each other to make meaning. Carly Spina (2021), a multilingual learner specialist and author, suggests asking students to *set intentions* for reading as part of the pre-reading process and having students reflect on what they read and what languages they read in.

Please ensure students get guided time to activate and/or build background knowledge of any text they are expected to care about. Neural pathways in our brains are built by connecting ideas together. Therefore, as educators, we must create tangible ways for all our students to connect to any given text or task. That's what an inclusive, equitable classroom needs. That's what all students deserve.

In a high school content classroom in which I have spent a considerable amount of time coaching, the teacher added a picture-walk element through student discussion before they tackled the heavy textbook (*literally* heavy and *figuratively* heavy, too!). The gains in student comprehension and engagement were tangible compared to when he simply told them to read the text without any time to preview, predict, and connect background knowledge with each other. Like many, if not all, of the practices presented in this guide, this one is not just for elementary students. I've seen firsthand how doing a quick picture walk to pre-read key pieces of information text in many middle and high school classrooms makes a huge difference for students!

A Couple Words about Reading Instruction

I'm going to put on my reading specialist hat for a moment and share a few words about teaching reading. These days, we have a hot debate about *the science of reading* that is influencing state and district policies, never mind the profits of many educational publishers. I'm old enough to remember that last time the field of education had a reading war, too! Getting into how to teach specific literacy skills or how to implement reading intervention methods is beyond the scope of this book. Yet when it comes to ensuring that our MLLs and our ALLs have the skills to read, including phonemic awareness, phonics, vocabulary, comprehension, and fluency, we need to take an individualized approach, not a prescriptive, one-size-fits-all approach. This may look different from student to student, from classroom to classroom. Recent research has found that many schools aren't necessarily considering MLLs' specific needs when teaching reading (Schwartz, 2022). Implementation matters; as I like to say, *it's about people, not just programs.*

When educators ask for my input, I explain that I do not endorse having younger students who are learning English mainly by interacting with sounds and words completely in isolation. The brain needs context, especially when learning a new language. Clapping out syllables within random words won't necessarily mean the same for a brain learning English as an additional language as it will for a student who only knows English. I also do not endorse multilingual students of any age (or any ALL student of any age, for that matter) blindly clicking through a reading program on a device as a *substitute* for literacy instruction or, at the very least, how to read closely and garnish meaning from a text. As I said at the start of our journey together, what works is high tech *and* high touch. I'll say the same about phonics and comprehension. We need both, not one at the expense of the other. In fact, we also need oral language development alongside literacy development. For example, cold reading alone doesn't work for many students. Neither do sounds or words floating in isolation without any context to ground them or reason to remember them for the transfer of skills, especially in a new language.

What I do endorse is: Discussions about the meaning and background knowledge activation/building, along with expanding oral language skills *alongside* foundational literacy skills like building phonemic awareness. It's not enough to only teach the words students will encounter in text, especially for MLLs. We may need a more customized approach for various learning profiles. Context matters, culture matters, and more holistic methods of literacy development are what educators should consider, not just for early learners but for older learners as well. If a student struggles with written print, let's remember that they may succeed through other channels like social contexts exceptionally well, and we should refrain from solely defining a student based on a label around achievement (Muhammad, 2020). Make the text meaningful; after all, as we have explored throughout this book, language is much more than the sounds it makes. Language is *cultural,* language is *fluid,* language is *interactive.*

Integrating All Domains through Purposeful Learning

Language learners benefit from rich instructional tasks that weave together listening, speaking, reading, and writing, which can—and I would say, *should*—revolve around meaningful, project-based learning. Students really benefit from knowing *why* we are learning something, and what better *why* than having it lead to something beyond not only the *sit-and-get* kind of instruction of old but also going beyond the traditional pen-and-paper test!

Let me give you an example. When I was teaching students as a fourth-grade classroom teacher, I taught thematically so that our units of study focused on an essential question. For example, *Why do people migrate?* was a major unit in my fourth-grade classroom in Milwaukee, integrating language arts, math, social studies, and the arts. We built a timeline of immigration in Wisconsin to guide our learning right along the classroom wall. We read passages from the social studies text and trade books at different Lexile levels for my diverse student readers, many of whom were multilingual. We watched videos, analyzed art, and had guest speakers and musicians from the community. At the beginning of the year, I inventoried students based on their preferred ways to learn and their interests, so I tried to provide opportunities for reading, writing, listening, and speaking in every lesson and ways to integrate acting, music, dance, and such. Suffice it to say my classroom was extremely interactive and full of creativity!

There was a lot of choice and reflection that the students partook in. The unit's final project was an *About My Family* book that had students research their own genealogy and express their story through photographs and art, which we then shared with the family and community. And you'd better believe I modeled it all along the way as best as possible by sharing and writing about my own family history. The project was also featured on Milwaukee Public Television's Spanish-language channel, so I had the pleasure of watching me teach in English with Spanish subtitles! Talk about meaningful learning for the students (and for me). Having multiple audiences for students' projects really boosted their purpose for learning. This was a lesson I took with me into every learning situation since. Make tasks meaningful and use the power of authentic assessment to motivate students and prepare them for life outside of school.

Critical Literacy Skills

With the demands of living and learning in our global society, it's becoming increasingly critical that we think of literacy as more than the basic or mechanical components of phonemic awareness, phonics, vocabulary, fluency, and comprehension. We also need to attend to the deeper, more nuanced, and complex competencies of interacting with various texts using critical interpretation skills and argumentation (Lesaux, Galloway, & Marietta, 2016). Let's take the earlier example I gave about the unit on Wisconsin indigenous history and family timelines in my classroom. One of our guest speakers in our classroom was an Ojibwe man who shared his special heirloom drum. Before the man came to my classroom, students shared some preconceived notions of what an indigenous man would look like before he visited our classroom. After his visit, we debriefed the experience, discussing their expectations versus what they experienced in reality. Many students shared that their only view of what *a person of Indian descent* looked like was what they saw on cartoons, in stereotypical tribal garb. My students hadn't had experiences beyond that. This new information greatly shaped their thinking, and I wanted to give them time to process that by researching other ways of viewing Native Americans. This experience spurred a longer-term series of teachable moments about *stereotyping* and *critical literacy*.

As Sara K. Ahmed (2018), a practitioner and author who focuses on identity and social comprehension, says, "Through [students'] questions, disagreements, and dialogue, they can negotiate meaning from multiple perspectives, including their own" (p. 77). Bringing critical literacy skills into our classrooms helps students take more ownership of their learning and allows meaningful language practice.

More Integration across the Language Domains

Not every unit can be as thematic as the one I described above for many reasons outside our control. However, can you think of ways to integrate your instruction across the language domains, making it more meaningful for students? Can you integrate technology and other tools to promote more student ownership, choice, multimodalities, and connection to the world outside your classroom? We will explore more ideas for project-based learning as it relates to assessment in Chapter 5. For now, I hope that this chapter on integrating the four domains of language has got you thinking about what you're currently doing in this area of the language lens and what you could try going forward! You could take stock of what your go-to activities are in each domain and discover what you're already doing and what areas you could improve so that in every lesson, your students can have both input and output experiences that engage across all domains of language. Good luck!

~

TIPS FOR TEACHERS: HOW DO WE ENSURE LANGUAGE/LITERACY-RICH LEARNING SPACES FOR ALL LEARNERS?

1. Be honest with yourself. What is your ratio of teacher talk to student talk? Track your ratio. Could it be improved? Also, can you break it down into *student-to-teacher and student-to-student talk*? Are students speaking in only one-word answers? Could you ask them to answer in complete sentences? What about students speaking to each other?

Could this be improved so that all students have increased opportunities to extend their discourse with one another in structured and supportive ways? What oral language activities, including academic conversations through group work protocols, do you currently have in your classroom? Are you calling on the same students all the time? Whose voices are not being heard? In reviewing the ideas in this chapter, what could you add to your toolbox to help facilitate more oral language in your classroom?

2. What is the role of literacy in your classroom? When are students expected to write, and what supports do they have to write effectively? When are they expected to read, and what supports do they have to read effectively? In reviewing the ideas in this chapter, what activities do you already have in your toolbox around literacy in your classroom? What could you add to your toolbox to help facilitate more literacy across your content area?

3. Are there ways you can collaborate with your content team members, your language specialist, and/or a coach to have a more consistently language- and literacy-rich classroom? Here are some ideas to do on your own or with a team:

4. Canvass your team or school to see the go-to strategies for bringing in each domain. Consider a quick survey or work with a coach or language specialist to see common reading, writing, listening, and speaking practices. If there are school or district improvement goals regarding focus strategies to bring a common instructional framework to life, that is also a great place to start. Ask your principal or other instructional leader what his or her vision of language and literacy across the curriculum is and see how that administrator can help bring more cohesion to how the system approaches the new standards with a language lens.

. . .

5. Create a language and literacy strategy bank with the team's or school's strategies so that you are all using a common toolbox. That way, you can capitalize on learning from one another—what works, what preparation is needed, what to prepare, and the like. Don't reinvent the wheel! Using technology like shared documents and folders can help you work smarter, not harder. You can also help students by assisting them to learn ways to engage in reading, writing, listening, and speaking in fun, systematic ways across themes, content areas, and instructors.

6. Reflect on a typical lesson and how long is spent on teacher-directed work, and how much is spent on student practice. You could even have a colleague observe you to provide that perspective. Put yourself in your students' shoes and think about what you would need to process new information using listening, speaking, reading, and writing strategies. You can even annotate your lesson plans and unit plans with reading, writing, listening, and speaking to indicate when students are engaged in each domain. Try to be sure that each domain is engaged in some respect in each learning experience from the students' perspective.

~

TIPS FOR COACHES AND LEADERS: HOW DO WE SUPPORT EDUCATORS IN THEIR DEVELOPMENT OF INCLUSIVE, ENGAGING, LANGUAGE-RICH CLASSROOMS?

1. This chapter dug into equity of voice in the classroom. Real-time coaching data is one of our most powerful tools as instructional leaders to move the needle here. Whether you are a coach or evaluator, you are in an influential role to collect, share and analyze coaching data that can transform how students interact in all classrooms. When you are observing instruction, quantify student voice. How do we do this? There are various ways. Here are some ideas to get you started:

- Tally the number of times students speak in a lesson
- Keep track, founding up to the minute, of teacher talk versus student talk
- Calculate the percentage of time the students spoke versus the total amount of time the teacher spoke
- Track which students are called on and which students are not, considering if any confirmation bias may be at play; for example, a teacher might think, *that student is hesitant to speak aloud in the whole group*, but if they never get called on, might we be reinforcing this assumption that the student won't or can't speak? Use real-time classroom coaching data to nudge educators past these mindsets.
- Go deeper by calculating the amount of student-to-teacher talk versus student-to-student talk
- Go deeper by tallying how much students spoke in words/phrases, complete sentences and discourse (multiple sentences). Share this data in your debrief to prompt shifts in mindset and practice. See the articles about data and inquiry at languagelens.com.

2. As we have touched on, parallel practices are important for equity-based schooling and professional learning spaces. Watch leader talk versus teacher talk in your school. Is there a teacher's voice? Is there equity of voice among your staff, or are all the same players steering the ship? Is your school a space where everyone has a seat at the table, or is it more about "my way or the highway"? Are you modeling risk-taking within a culture of learning, or are you enforcing that you have all the answers? In other words, are you modeling and expecting the same practices in the classroom and your professional learning? If not, please do. What works in the classroom with students also works when working with adult learners.

. . .

3. The concept of "chunk and chew" is a big part of the language lens. This means, as this chapter explained that we bring in all domains of language in lessons so that students can listen, speak, read, and write, enabling them to process information, not just passively input it. Learning should be meaningful and even joyful! Take stock of your role as a professional learning coach and/or facilitator. Once again, are you modeling this in your PD? Or are you unwittingly asking staff to obtain information by drinking through a proverbial firehose, where it would be better processed through more of a drinking fountain (or bubbler!) approach? How do you check educators' understanding, especially in coaching/feedback situations? Giving feedback isn't going to necessarily make the shift in the classrooms we want. We can have educators co-create their own goals and next steps, chunking and chewing the next steps incrementally. Where are you succeeding with those you support in processing information effectively? Where could you improve?

CHAPTER 5
SCAFFOLDS FOR INPUT AND OUPUT

THIS CHAPTER FOCUSES ON THE LANGUAGE LENS COMPETENCY OF supporting language development: providing scaffolds for input and output as part of teaching and assessing.

- ESSENTIAL QUESTION FOR ALL EDUCATORS, ESPECIALLY TEACHERS: How Will You Add to Your Toolbox So That You Can Implement Language Routines and Scaffolds?
- ESSENTIAL QUESTIONS FOR COACHES/LEADERS: How Do We Sustain and Scale Systemic Practices for Maximum Impact Across Our Schools?

In this final chapter of our journey through the language lens, we will put all of the pieces together from the previous chapter so that instruction and assessment can be scaffolded for all language learners. Content teachers can support academic language development by providing interactive tools that scaffold both the instruction (input) and assessment (output) for learners. Throughout this chapter, I will present activities for teaching and learning that you may want to choose from to add to your toolbox.

In the journey of learning, it's important to have tools along the way. If you're driving a car in a new state or country, for example, you would likely have navigation tools to support you, if they were available. I know *I* use them! How else would one know the way without directions, a map, or road signs? And what if you don't speak the language of this new place? Certainly, you'd need ways to understand what's going on, or you may never reach your destination.

GPS as a Scaffold

In my world of consulting with schools and organizations, I often have to get myself to a new location by car, train, or plane. I constantly think about how much of a savior the GPS app on my smartphone is for travel and how grateful I am for this technology. If I'm going to a place for the first time, I rely heavily on GPS support. The next time I go, I may refer to it less.

Then, if I go to this place frequently, I may have GPS support available but not rely on it because I've learned the way by paying attention to the signs, the landmarks, and such. However, I'll be the first to admit that I am often over-reliant on this technology, so I don't have to learn the way! I am not putting forth the effort to really put this route into my longer-term memory. I know, in these cases, that I'm using this tool as a *crutch*, not a *scaffold*! Scaffolds and supports are meant to be removed to build independence when we are ready as learners.

For our language learners, the journey of learning new content is no different. Try to put yourself in their shoes and predict what tools or scaffolds they will need to have along the way. Our multilingual learners are learning both language and content, so you must think of both.

As you have been learning about the language lens through this guide, you may have noticed that I've provided many tools for you in this book. Tools like diagrams, bolded terms, scenarios, examples, and other key features have been integrated because they help with learning. Imagine if I just gave you the theories behind language acquisition without any explanation or opportunities to make it more real, more accessible for you as an educator. You may recall experiences in your career where you tuned out professional development because there were no clear signposts, directions, clear expectations, and other scaffolds. You may yourself have been the disenfranchised student! We do not want that happening to our students or learners of any age. We do not want our learners to be tuning out and becoming disengaged in learning. So how do we use our language lens to build the appropriate scaffolds for our students in our content classrooms?

Input and Output from Students' Perspective

The first thing I recommend is thinking about what happens in your classrooms as input and output from students' perspectives. In the last chapter, we unpacked the language domains—reading, writing, listening, and speaking. Well, if you think about it in terms of the domains of language, what students are hearing (or listening to) and reading comprises input. What students are discussing (or speaking about) and writing comprises output. As Figure 5.1 represents, the input is what the learner's brain receives, while the output is what the learner expresses.

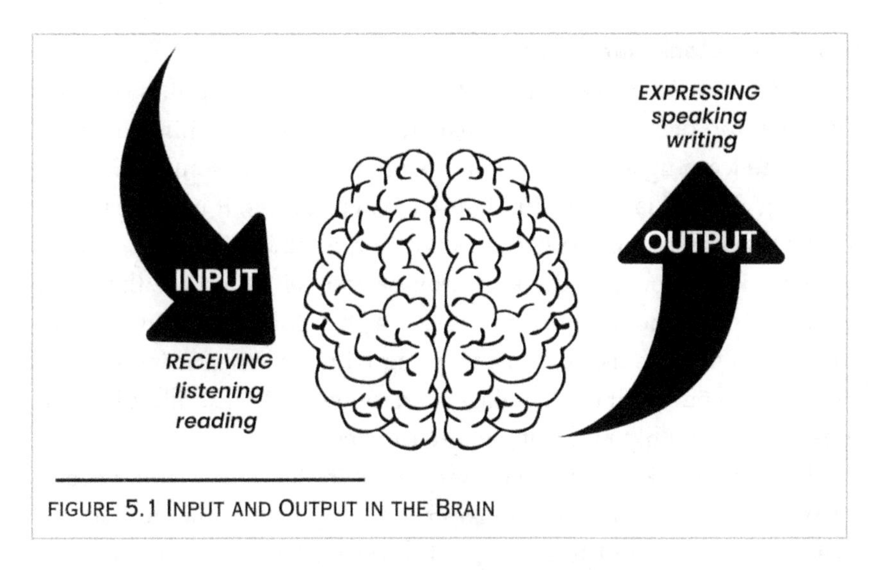

FIGURE 5.1 INPUT AND OUTPUT IN THE BRAIN

As a teacher, you're teaching and assessing. What you're presenting or facilitating in your classroom regarding what students hear and read is what we will refer to as input. What you're assessing of student understanding through their speaking and writing is what we will refer to as output. A pioneer in the field of second language acquisition, Stephen Krashen, conceptualized the key theory of the input hypothesis (as cited in Schütz, 2017). which basically states that students need to have access to *comprehensible input* through meaningful communication, not the memorization of grammar rules or other aspects of language in isolation. In other words, if we are learning a new language, we need to understand the *gist* of what is being communicated, or the main message, not necessarily every detail. In this way, learning a new language is very parallel to when we learn our first language. We are given messages in context, not lessons on how to get subject-verb agreement. When language is taught in comprehensible ways through appropriate scaffolds, we are actually putting students in a position to acquire language. We are providing opportunities for students to be in the flow of learning, as opposed to a more formal or rigid language teaching situation.

Making Messages Meaningful

To illustrate the importance of ensuring that our input is comprehensible for our students, I'd like to invite you to think about a language learning experience you may have had. For some, it may be learning a world language in high school. For others, it may be a more contextual experience of living or visiting another linguistic setting, whether it be a neighborhood nearby or another country. Either way, recall what was not helpful and what was helpful for you. In terms of being helpful, cues like visuals, working with a partner, using translations from your heritage language, and, in general, meaningful activities that stick with you go into long-term memory.

For me, I think about when I was living in Puerto Rico and needed to purchase a mop at the grocery store for my new home in this new place. Before I set out to the store, I retrieved the word for *mop* from my Spanish instruction way back in high school, *el trapeador*, just in case I needed it, although I figured I would easily find the cleaning supplies section in the store and that I wouldn't need to communicate much aside from checking out with the cashier. I had only been in Puerto Rico for a day or two and was awash with the mixed emotions of this-is-all-so-exciting-yet-terrifying that many newcomers at any age feel in the beginning stages of being in a new culture and language.

At the store, I couldn't find the cleaning supplies area, so I needed to ask for help. I was so excited to put together a request in the form of a question to a store employee and did so with perfect grammar: *¿Disculpeme, dónde puedo encontrar un trapeador?* (Excuse me, where can I find a mop?) The employee looked at me blankly even after I tried the translation of the sentence in English. I panicked at first yet, then started to act out what one does with this cleaning tool, leaning over and grabbing an imaginary mop to pretend-clean the grocery store floor in earnest. Still, the blank look from the clerk. I tried to speak again, using the communication strategy known as *circumlocution,* where you talk about the term without actually using the term, in Spanish; that made me feel and sound like a four-year-old: *You know, the thing one uses to floor . . . I mean, clean floor. Are things at this store?* Finally, the clerk's face lit up in recognition. *Aha! Un mopo!*

Now, it may go without saying that the Spanish I learned in high school was from Spain, not from Latin America, and more specifically, not from Puerto Rico. That whole experience would have gone a lot more smoothly for me if I had known that I was in a very different language learning experience, one that relied more on English than I anticipated. Like many places in the world, the impact of English as a global language can be heard and seen. What's more, Puerto Rico is part of the United States. So, like many other colonized places, the linguistic echo can be heard as the various languages have been intertwined over time. All to say, the Spanish instruction I had in high school did not necessarily give me the right language for this cultural context. We mainly studied Spanish from Spain in isolation through grammar translation activities and games so that, even after three years of study, I was still an early intermediate language learner, as I demonstrated by speaking in short sentences and only understanding words, phrases, and chunks of language I read or heard.

Scaffolding Language Interactions

You might, as I did at first, find it fascinating that the clerk at the market didn't recognize the word *mop* when I spoke it in English. However, when you consider that the vowel sound *o* is very different in the English word *mop* (short o) from the Spanish word *mopo* (long o), you may better understand the confusion. At any rate, I share this story to demonstrate the power of making messages meaningful by purposefully using scaffolds to make the messages comprehensible. I scaffolded my language input for the store employee by trying to describe what it was using other words, by using an exact translation, and by gesturing (lots of gestures!). Believe me, I will never forget the term *el mopo* because the experience itself was unforgettable! For our students, we want exciting, meaningful learning experiences in the safe space of our content classrooms, where they can learn about a concept, a new skill, and/or knowledge with meaning and support. We want to provide helpful scaffolds and give students something to hang on to, so they can make sense of what they are learning.

Beware of Over- and Under-Scaffolding

Remember how I shared that I use the scaffold of my GPS tool when driving to a new place? Well, I also admitted that I am often over-reliant on my GPS as well. I could certainly work to internalize the route to a place I go to frequently, but I tend to let the tool rescue me so that I don't have to really learn my way without the tool. I let it guide me so I don't have to do the deeper work! You see, a scaffold is a support that may be taken away over time. When a house is built, for example, scaffolds are there to support the building of the house but are taken down once the house is built. If we take the concept of what a scaffold actually is to our classroom, we want to be purposeful in using scaffolds so that students have them as support when needed.

Under-scaffolding is when we don't provide enough supports for students to make meaning out of what we are teaching or how students are being assessed. What does this look like? One example is Scenario A: a classroom where students are passively listening to a lecture for the entire class period. There are no visible student tools for them to interact with. Another example is Scenario B: when a student receives an exam that has them write a five-paragraph essay about the causes of the American Revolution. There is no evidence of writing scaffolds in the exam or nearby for the student to refer to, simply the writing prompt. When this happens, Scenario A becomes solely a function of the students' listening proficiency, and in Scenario B, the social studies test has become a writing test instead. Neither scenario is language-rich in terms of providing scaffolds for students to get the input to learn, and neither validly assesses their output. In other words, students are not necessarily set up for success, and so *what exactly are we assessing in this case*, I ask?

Stay in the Challenge Zone

On the other hand, over-scaffolding can look like providing too much support, and yes, there is such a thing! Sometimes I go into classrooms where students have a barrage of scaffolds to the point that they don't have to take risks outside their comfort zones to try out new learning. For example, students learning through a science experiment may simply copy the exact language and content they need from the lab sheet without producing any new language of their own when they are perfectly capable of it. This is not to say that beginning English learners do not benefit from copying because they certainly can. Copying is a way to learn a new language by reproducing it so long as it is attached to meaning!

We don't want to lower the bar so low that we enact what some call the *pobrecito* approach for language learners. *Pobrecito* in Spanish means *poor little thing*, and this approach can often shelter too much for students so they don't need to do much or any work outside of their *zone of actual development*. We want to keep learning in the challenge zone, also known as the *zone of proximal development* (McLeod, 2018). We are not doing students any favors when we don't challenge them and "water down" high standards. We are actually doing students a major disservice by widening the opportunity gap of them not having access to what they deserve. With a *pobrecito* mindset, we may be unable to see students' agency in their own learning and story. This choice we have as educators is exemplified by educator and author

Emily Francis (2022) here in this letter to one of her students with interrupted education, Marco:

When I first heard your story, I had two options. I could have felt bad for you. I could've pitied you for being so young and feeling like you couldn't continue your education. Or, I could have done what I decided to do instead: praise you for the difficult decisions you've made. Because I had seen your strength, I was so excited to…tell you how amazed I am by the way you've created the life you think is best for yourself (p. 84)

We can imagine how Marco's experience in school was so positively impacted by his teacher's choice to respect him, challenge him, and support the vision of himself he was working towards. Likewise, we can also imagine if Marco's teacher had had a deficit view of him and lowered the bar, expecting him to not go far. Students really sense how we feel about them, so, like Mrs. Francis did with Marco, let's make sure we foster students' beliefs in themselves.

As Stephen Krashen teaches, as part of his *input hypothesis*, we need to acknowledge the language level of the student and then go slightly above it to challenge them and help them extend their language development, also called input plus one or i + 1. So when you think about your learners, especially your English learners, first consider their zone of actual development, which is where they are now. This means knowing their holistic language level, as shown in Chapter 1, plus it means that we also consider their social-emotional needs, interests, and general readiness to learn, all factors we discussed in Chapter 2. Then consider what level of support they may benefit from, keeping in mind that the amount of scaffolding should decrease with the more English proficiency the students acquire, although many scaffolds for input and output support ALL learners! Bottom line, we want to challenge students, not over-scaffold. Life, after all, isn't over-scaffolded, is it? We typically have to find our own way, so we want our students to develop language, literacy, and *life* skills.

The Art of Differentiation

Before we explore the various kinds of scaffolds that enrich instruction and make our messages more meaningful, I'd like to clarify that there is no one way to provide scaffolds in a content classroom. Each classroom is different because its students are unique, as is their teacher or teachers, as well as the local community and curriculum at hand. Often, educators ask me, *What is the best way to differentiate for language learners?* I will tell you what I tell them: Differentiation means we have to respond to the students in front of us. There is no one way to do it. We need to design instruction that meets students' needs as best we can, given the tools we have at the time, and *teach them how to learn,* or better yet, *teach them how to teach themselves.* As Hattie (2023) explains, "A critical skill is teaching students the skills of detecting the nature of success of the learning desired and knowing where they are in the learning cycle so they better optimize the choice of teaching and learning strategies—this is the essence of self-regulation" (p. 352). To me, this is the essence of learning and living!

As we plan, teach, and assess, we want to keep in mind that differentiated teaching is an art, and arts are partly learned skills and partly connecting with students in real-time, students from many different linguistic and cultural groups. In this chapter, my goal is to give you ideas for scaffolding your differentiated classroom of language learners. Some ideas can be planned ahead; others need to be enacted in the moment.

Some may not work for your setting, and some may not be in this toolbox here. Your job is to reflect on what you currently do, what the needs of your students are, and what you can take with you going forward to refine your practice. We call teaching a practice for a reason! Like artists always honing their craft, we, as teachers, are always learning and growing in response to the students in front of us.

Student Ownership of Learning

We want the right amount of challenge to allow students to do the deeper work over time to put learning into longer-term memory. As we know, in a differentiated classroom, that can look different for each group of students or each student individually, which is why it's important to talk about the power of student ownership, sometimes called student agency, in learning.

What do I mean by student ownership? As I touched on in the previous chapter, student ownership means that students have a voice and choice in their learning. They are not passive recipients of what teachers transmit to them but are instead active participants in constructing their own knowledge. When I support teachers, coaches, and leaders, one of the primary places I start is by asking students about their experiences at school. When we ask students about their school experiences, we hear how effective or ineffective we are right from the end user. The end user is who the service is designed for, much like I am the end user of the GPS app on my smartphone. The app would not be useful to me if it showed me the software code that designed it. The app is only useful to me in terms of how user-friendly it is and how functional it is as a value-add to my navigation experience. So, like an app on a smartphone, we want to design learning with the end user's experience front and center. As illustrated in Figure 5.2, we want students to take charge of their learning, to enjoy learning, and to really, truly benefit from the learning experiences we create for them. Some general ideas for implementing more student ownership in your classroom include:

- Group work so the teacher is not the only one talking or conveying knowledge to students
- Choices for assessments, not just the traditional pen-and-paper test
- Student-generated goals and expectations co-generated with the teacher(s) on language, effort, behavior, and so on
- Student self-assessment and peer-assessment of learning processes and products using rubrics, checklists, and goal-setting
- Shout-outs where students get to point out positive behaviors or skills of other students
- Having students choose work samples to keep in a portfolio, celebrating growth over time

- Representations of different identity groups in texts and visuals (race, ethnicity, class, language, religious affiliation, gender identity, sexual orientation, ability, immigration status)
- Practicing critical literacy skills by looking at multiple perspectives in texts and the author's purpose

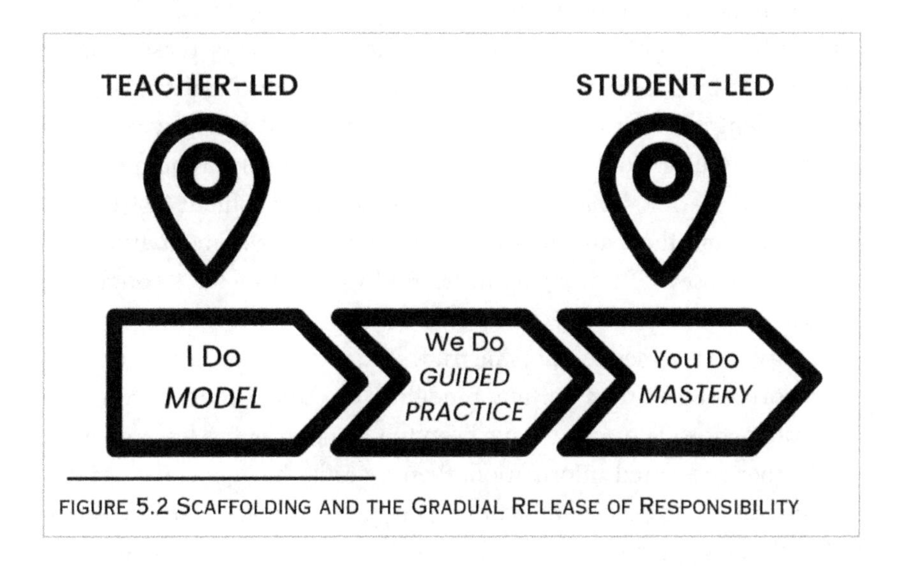

FIGURE 5.2 SCAFFOLDING AND THE GRADUAL RELEASE OF RESPONSIBILITY

Scaffolds for MLLs and for ALLs

When reviewing the following collection of scaffolding ideas, be sure to keep in mind that many scaffolds are great for all learners. In my work training and coaching with the language lens, I hear from educators often, *What works for MLLs is just* good teaching! This is partly true. While what can work for MLLs can also work well for ALLs, we do need to be aware that MLLs require specific attention to their linguistic and cultural needs and assets. As I discussed earlier in this guide, our attention to language proficiency level and cultural aspects is critical. At the same time, when we become more intentional about planning, teaching, and assessing with a language lens, we make our whole classroom more language-rich and metacognitive, which is great for every learner! So, as I share the following scaffolding ideas with you, please consider which scaffolds you currently use or could use for specific needs and which could be effective for your entire classroom.

The Gradual Release of Responsibility

You may be familiar with the concept of the gradual release of responsibility, or GRR (see Figure 5.2), where the teacher presents new information by modeling, then guided practice is implemented before independent work or assessment, is expected. GRR is a way to think about how we scaffold content for all our students. In a moment, we will look at scaffolds that support GRR in terms of content instruction and assessment that can also scaffold language development. But first, let's unpack how GRR is a way to scaffold for all students through the *I do, We do, You do* process.

All too often, I see teachers instruct students to engage in independent work without much or any modeling or guided practice through peer interaction. There may have been the *I do* part of the lesson where the teacher presented information, then there is the *You do* part of the lesson where students are all working on their own on a task or a set of tasks. What happened to the middle part of the gradual release of responsibility—the *We do?* Modeling with students and structuring student-to-student interaction facilitates deeper learning. This guided practice part of the lesson gives each student a chance to "demonstrate their grasp of new learning under the teachers' direct supervision," where the teacher provides feedback and supports individuals as needed (Hattie, 2023, p. 361). It's like you taught someone to ski by first telling them about skiing, having them watch you ski, and then sending them down the mountain without any support along the way, saying, *Good luck!* We might as well say, *If you don't learn, it's not my fault!* Common sense tells us this would be unlikely to work and could even injure the person learning to ski. Wouldn't it also injure your ego as teacher? I feel the best evidence that we taught something well is if the students can show us that they learned it. Therefore, I invite you to think of any learning situation as just as critical as sending someone down a ski hill without the appropriate guided practice and feedback to improve.

Without the *We do* part of the lesson structure, one of two things can happen. First, what can happen is an unspoken vow of silence in the classroom where students are expected to learn simply by thinking inside their own heads, only asking for support from the teacher if they are brave enough. The other thing that can happen is that students are anything but silent. Students display off-task chitchat, and many try to fool the teacher into thinking they are actually working. Many students aren't getting the support they need, so they avoid working. *Who wouldn't?* I ask. It's like going to a workshop for educators where the facilitator employs this *spray and pray* approach where they ask you to listen, almost praying that hearing their ideas is enough to actually learn and apply these ideas. The brain needs stimulation, practice, and interaction, so let's make sure we plan for that in our lessons and professional learning spaces. As we reviewed in Chapter 4, stop *ping-ponging* across from one student to another and build in more learner-led structures to facilitate discussions and the application of learning.

One quick example is when introducing a text, why not model the fluency and new words, phrases, and sentences by reading the sentences aloud? Then, have students read chorally just as you did so no "round robin" or "cold calling" has to happen. While cold calling may work for some tasks, please don't put students on the spot if they are not set up to be successful with the language. For students new to English, their oral language proficiency may be more proficient than their literacy, so teachers can take advantage of this through choral reading (DeCapua, Marshall, Tang, 2020). *Choral reading* and *choral response* can also be very effective in getting all students to use language without putting one student on the spot. The teacher can model fluency or have a student or a group of students lead by example. Having students speak and/or read aloud chorally is a great way to add speaking and reading in ways that scaffold the language for all learners.

In listening to some teachers I coach, I hear that many are so focused on the endpoint of covering the curriculum that this becomes the primary focus. Educators often wonder aloud, *I taught it. Why didn't they learn it?* When, in fact, the question could instead be, *In seeing that students didn't learn from my teaching, what can I do to more effectively reach and teach them?* I urge you to slow down to ensure that students actually process the information so that they truly will remember it. Chunk, chew and check for understanding!

As the saying goes, *Sometimes you have to go slow to go fast.* By this, I mean when you take the time to ensure students have adequate practice with supports, the payoff will be bigger in the end. Students will learn what you are covering when you make the time and space—and scaffolds!—for them to engage in deeper, more relevant, student-centered learning. Part of each lesson should also include intentional time for closure, not just ending class surprisingly when the bell rings. As educators, we need to create space for closure of the lesson, clarifying any misunderstandings, providing feedback, and making the learning cohesive for students; "simply asking, 'Any questions? No, OK, let's move on' is not closure" (Hattie, 2023, p. 361). When we make the invisible aspects of language more visible through intentional lesson design, our students—MLLs and ALLs—benefit. But how do we make the language of thinking in your content classroom visible to students? Let's go through some key scaffolds content teachers can use to support both input and output in their classrooms.

General Language Scaffolds for ALLs

Because language is a key aspect of any content classroom, I recommend that all educators take stock of how they use the following scaffolds and activities so that students have access to them should they need them. Because student ownership is a major focus of the language lens, please consider how students are choosing to use—or not use—these supports. I work with many schools where scaffolds like these are available for all learners, yet, because not all learners need them at any given time, the onus is on the student to use them. I find power in having students reflect on what supports they used—or didn't use—when performing a task to boost metacognition, metalinguistic awareness, or their own language lens as they learn. This is the power of choice. As you read this list, consider what you currently use and what you could try:

A. Maximize your classroom's "real estate" so that students are deeply engaged in learning.

A classroom is for student learning, and its design should reflect the end-user experience. I've been in hundreds of classrooms at all grade levels, and how a classroom is configured is a direct reflection of the values of the teacher in terms of how students can and should learn.

If the teacher's desk is front and center with rows for students to sit and listen passively, then that's what will happen. Conversely, if a classroom has students' desks configured in small groups, then we could expect cooperative learning to occur. When I see blank walls or walls peppered with store-bought motivational signs, I wonder what opportunities students have to share their learning with one another or what tools they can access to structure and scaffold content. If shelves have easily accessible materials for students to access and walls remind students of the topics at hand through co-created anchor charts and student work, I can see that the instruction is likely to be more student-centered and learner-led.

This is not to say that a blank space cannot be conducive to learning. It can. Plus, many teachers have to travel or share space. Trust me, I've had to be a traveling teacher and make something out of nothing in many spaces. I've had so many back-of-the-library and hallways spaces that have been extremely unideal for student learning. A lot of times, the conditions of the space in which we teach are out of our control, yet the energy and materials a teacher can bring into any room, or part of a room you may be sharing, can make or break what students get from your instruction. So please don't underestimate how an inviting classroom can promote deep, collaborative learning and how the classroom itself is a tool or set of tools for students to use to succeed.

. . .

B. Teach vocabulary in interesting and effective ways.

Did you know that looking words up in a glossary or dictionary doesn't lead to student retention of these words (Duke, 2016)? Students need to work with words in context and use them over and over again, not just regurgitate a surface-level definition. There are so many interactive ways to teach vocabulary!

Two of my favorites for content teachers are the Seven Step Vocabulary Method and TPR. The Seven Step Vocabulary Method, conceptualized by Margarita Calderon (2007), is a structured way to teach new words to students beyond the definition. Here are the general steps:

1. The teacher says the words, and the students repeat the word up to three times. This is often referred to as *choral response* or *choral reading*.
2. The teacher reads a sentence with the word in it for context.
3. The teacher gives the dictionary or glossary definition.
4. The teacher explains the word using student-friendly definitions.
5. The teacher highlights aspects of the word that can be challenging for students.
6. The teacher engages students in an oral language activity using the word.
7. The teacher provides a task where the students are using the word through reading and writing.

Many teachers I know take this protocol and adapt it for their classroom and their own teaching style, which I highly recommend, so long as it meets the needs of your students. I happen to think that having students create their own definitions for step 4 is key; plus, allowing them to share what it is in their heritage language or languages is also very important. Drawing it out and/or adding a gesture (à la TPR) is also effective for many brains.

Total physical response, or TPR, was conceptualized by James Asher in the 1970s, and it uses gestures to make a word come to life (Ludescher, 2018). I use it a lot, even when teaching adults. For example, when I teach the language domains, and we are talking about the input channels (listening and reading) and the output channels (speaking and writing), I will gesture using my hands to show the difference. For input, I will wave my hands toward my head to indicate that information is coming into my brain. For output, I will extend my hands to mean that I am expressing or sharing information. I will have the adult learners do the same. Through TPR, the brain has the opportunity to make more meaning because of body movement. The brain loves movement, along with rhyme, rhythm, and repetition! Make learning words fun by having students make up their own gestures, too.

C. Capitalize on cognates and word study.

We know that our multilingual learners come from many different language backgrounds and many different language families. What do I mean by language families? A group of related languages comprises a language family that comes from a common ancestral language, and there are known to be 147 language families in the world (Thompson, 2015). Indo-European languages like Greek, Slavic, and Roman languages come from similar roots yet have their own characteristics. When we teach students to look for these common roots, we use the strategy of discovering root words and even cognates.

Let's take the word assess in English, for example. Although it can be traced back to Middle English, it is likely rooted in the Latin word *assessus,* which is the past participle of the word *assidere,* which literally means "to sit beside." If we think about the spirit of assessment in its most authentic form, we hope to be learning about what a student can do by literally or figuratively sitting beside the student. Assessment, when done accurately, is an act that is something we do in service of students, although I'm sure you could argue, as can I, that assessment is often something that is done, especially large-scale assessments, not entirely in service of students and certainly not always in ways that accurately assess what students can do. At any rate, my point here is that by diving into the word history of the word assess, we can see that it is connected to the term to sit beside, not by accident. There is meaning there.

Another way to make words come to life is to teach cognates. For example, the word *sugar* in English is similar to the following:

- *zuker* in German
- *suiker* in Dutch
- *caxap* (pronounced *sakhar)* in Russian
- *azúcar* in Spanish
- *cukiar* in Polish
- *cukr* in Czech
- سكر (pronounced *sukar*) in Arabic

Approximately 30–40 percent of English words have a word that is similar in Spanish and other Latin-based languages, like *map/mapa, dollar/dólar,* and *camera/cámara,* to name a few (Colorin Colorado, 2017). Allow students to share the cognates they hear and read. Some teachers even co-create lists with students throughout the year. As previously mentioned in Chapter 3, I encourage you to check out Dr. Averil Coxhead's Academic Word List for an immensely useful collection of the top word families used across all academic settings (the website is listed in the Bibliography).

In word study, analyzing the parts of words, or morphemes, is an effective way to get students to see patterns and meaning across content areas (Ebbers, 2008). For example, if you teach that the prefix inter means *between,* students can see it in many words, like *international, interface, interstate, intertwine,* and *interval.* In fact, there are forty-five more words—at least!—that use this prefix (Sight Word Games, 2013). Talk about word power!

Word study and cognate study, in general, is an effective way to be more linguistically responsive through small steps. Before you think to yourself that you don't have time to do this, please consider that this can be integrated into what you already do with vocabulary. Remember, the language lens is not an add-on. I've seen teachers simply add this in by doing a quick word study for a few minutes once a week with content vocabulary related to the unit. Like all the ideas presented here, make it your own so that you and your students get excited about language and retain this learning!

. . .

D. Incorporate visuals.

For our visual learners and our language learners, using visuals is so important. Videos, pictures, drawings, and diagrams can make learning real for students, as well as what may also be referred to as *realia,* or actual objects from the real world. For example, when teaching about the Industrial Revolution, show images of the *locomotive* along with synonyms like *train.* When referring to a country, pull it up on a map. Perhaps also point to the flag. When connecting to a cultural concept like a fairy-tale character or a pop cultural icon, quickly bring up a picture online. Not all learners have the same cultural references, so please don't make assumptions that exclude some individuals or groups. Be aware of your *blind spots,* culturally speaking. Don't just talk or use text. Students need to see or connect to a new concept to activate prior learning if they already know it. As the saying goes, *A picture is worth a thousand words.* So when teaching about any given topic, please take a moment to see what visual cue or piece of realia can make the topic come alive!

E. Teach students to keep track of new language learned.

It's not enough to just hear new language and content. We must use it and, for many learners, keep track of it in a way that is meaningful to us personally. If you've ever studied a new language, you may have kept your own list of new words and phrases for extra practice and easy retrieval. Remember that the more we engage students across all domains of language—reading, writing, listening, and speaking—the better. Academic language journals can be a wonderfully supportive tool for content classrooms. You can use your own structure to create a template for students. More and more classrooms, not just elementary classrooms, are employing the use of language journals and word walls for student use. Have fun with language and consider ways to group words and phrases together by meaning, or have students create their own semantic groups to see what they find useful.

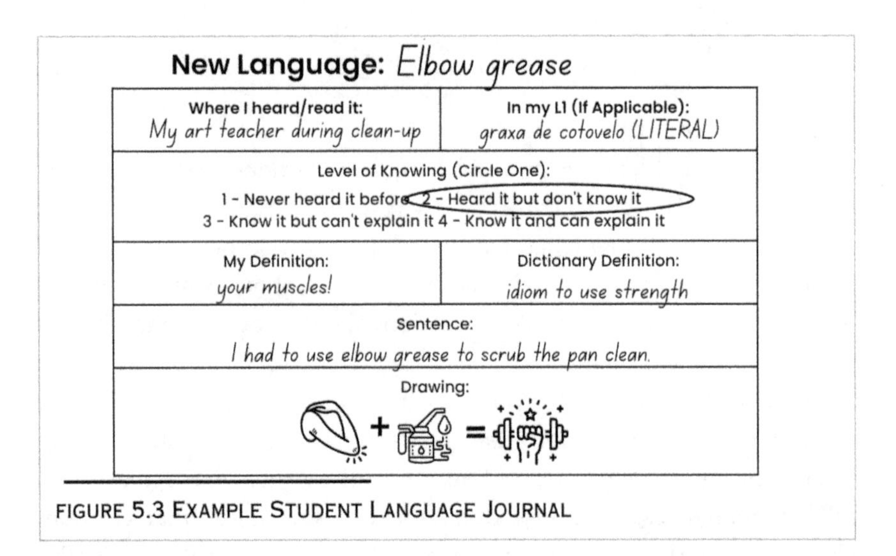

FIGURE 5.3 EXAMPLE STUDENT LANGUAGE JOURNAL

I always had my students use an academic language journal, much like the example I've created for you in Figure 5.3. Whether you use an interactive word wall or a 4-square vocabulary organizer/Freyer model, the goal is to encourage students to *own their language development.* In my example here, you can see the space for students to first identify where they heard or read this new language. I loved it when my students came into class in the morning excited to share new phrases or terminology they heard on the news or from an older sibling. Language isn't just what happens in school! If students have a home language other than English, have them write the translation or look up the translation with care, again remembering that not all MLL students have literacy in their home language. The levels of knowing bring students into the language development process because they identify how well they know or don't know that language which honors their background knowledge as a critical part of learning. The spaces for both a student-created definition and a dictionary or glossary definition help explain what the new language means. Remember that, as I shared earlier, that definitions alone do not foster long-term retention and usage. Furthermore, translation alone does not always work, as this example about *elbow grease* in Figure 5.3. shows. The brain needs meaning, so bringing in visuals and student-created sentences gives more context as students keep track—individually or as part of a whole class experience—of their own language.

F. Use—and model—student tools to set a learning purpose and structure thinking.

A major part of the language lens in content classrooms is making our thinking visible as we learn content. The language goals we create to guide student learning can be made visible through key student tools like graphic organizers, note-taking guides, and sentence frames that correspond to the language function. For instance, as you read this guide, these are our goals of this guidebook:

- Identify effective practices for language learners in content classrooms
- Analyze your current mindsets and practices so you can plan the next steps for improving your classroom

To *identify* and *analyze* effective practices you'd like to try, you might create a list or a chart as you move through this guide. You may have your own note-taking system in a notebook or an online document you're using as you move through this book. As discussed in Chapter 4, you may use your annotation system as you close read. You may jot down a graphic organizer of a list of what you're learning tied to a column of the next steps. Whatever system you use can help structure your thinking.

What's important is to show students that there are language structures behind language functions. Having the language scaffolds to hang that content learning on is important. Hence, students understand how to listen for that language and how to express that language, whether English is their first language or not. Modeling how to use the language by thinking aloud and/or writing the target language and content can really show students the thinking behind the learning! A note of caution here is to not only use sentence frames and only expect sentence frames. We want original language, too. The frames are a scaffold meant to model and provide a pathway to generate new language. We don't want to "cap" learning at these language frames, considering what we discussed earlier: *i + 1*. To see examples of the language structures behind language functions, go to languagelens.com and download Confianza's Language Functions Tool.

G. Start with the end of the unit in mind by creating study guides.

Just as it's important to tie together the language domains so students hear, speak, read, and write the target language and content in each lesson you're teaching, it's just as important that students know the goals and key pieces of language of the entire unit. Many teachers I work with find study guides very useful to present to students so they know what is happening in a unit. The idea is to provide students the whole road map for the unit. Some teachers question me when I suggest this, saying, *But aren't I giving students the answers?* And my response is generally that when we give students the appropriate tools, especially the language tools, we aren't necessarily giving them the answer because it's up to the students to engage with the language and to construct meaning out of it. We don't want assessment to be a guessing game for students, or *What are we learning and why?* or a *Gotcha* where students don't know what's coming. We want them to be prepared and, like a navigation system does as we drive in a new place, we want to let them know what's coming and how to zoom back and see the big picture of the journey.

The study guide can include the following components:

- The essential question(s) and big ideas for the unit
- The goals, including language goals
- Key words and phrases
- Sentence frames connected to the language function in the goals
- Visuals and graphic organizers for the language being used
- Key resources, including what texts are being referred to
- Information about the final project or assessment

. . .

H. Groups, groups, groups!

You've read several times in this guide how important groups are to students learning, and I'll say it again here. Consider what parts of your lesson would allow students to process information, apply new learning, and practice new skills more efficiently and effectively in cooperative groups. Students benefit when they are in charge of their learning and when they have active learning through peer interaction (Shen, 2018). Jigsaw reading, where students chunk a text and come together to build a common understanding is extremely effective, as is reciprocal teaching, where specific roles foster collective learning (Hattie, 2023). However, we need to be thoughtful about when, why, and how we engage students in group work. Reflect on the following tips to see where your practice might improve in terms of group work:

- Communicate that the function of group work is to build knowledge together but that becoming an effective group takes practice.
- Make sure students have a clear set of roles and routines for group work to be successful, e.g.:

Predictor: This person uses information from the text and the annotations made by his/her group members, to determine what will happen next in the text.

Summarizer: This person asks the group members to share what key ideas they found in the text. This person will then rephrase the text in his/her own words.

Questioner: This person asks other students to share their annotations on the text and why. This person can also ask questions to help the group better understand the text that has been read.

Clarifier: This person helps clarify the material being discussed in the text, whether it be vocabulary words or a confusing sentence.

- Practice how a group works functionally, including *fishbowling*, or model examples and non-examples of effective groups in front of the whole class to debrief what works and what doesn't work.
- Make sure it's clear that students are responsible for their individual learning *and* how the group learns collectively.
- Post group roles and expectations and allow students to self-assess and peer-assess on group functions. Reflection should be part of the classroom culture for every learner, including the teacher.
- Involve students in creating group norms and protocols. Refer back as necessary to provide feedback.
- Allow for differentiation for MLLs at more beginner levels of languages so they can listen more versus being in charge of facilitating group discussion.
- Give students the language tools already discussed in this chapter to hang their learning on, like graphic organizers, note-taking systems, and sentence frames for discussion.
- Match the purpose of the grouping to the way you group; heterogeneous by language proficiency level for practice could be one way, or homogeneous by language proficiency level for guided work with a teacher on specific needs could be another way to group.
- Use a simple class list as a formative checklist of desired behaviors for group work *and* for desired target language you'd like students to use, like the key vocabulary and whether or not students are speaking in complete sentences (provide sentence stems/frames for this purpose!).
- Plan performance-based assessments or projects using group work so students have the opportunity to work in structured ways with their peers; build multimodal ways for students to share their reports or projects using presentations, video, and other technologies.

Too often, in the classroom, I see well-intentioned teachers or co-teachers put students in groups or let students choose their own groups without guardrails in place. Students are left to their own devices to "work together" yet don't always know what working together looks, sounds, and feels like. They aren't set up for success, and so the teachers aren't either. Remember, it's about the *process* of learning. Make that process—and the language for it—visible!

Differentiating for MLLs, Especially Beginners

As mentioned earlier, beginning MLLs need more scaffolding than others who are further along in their language proficiency journey. That doesn't mean we put these students in situations where high standards aren't expected. Sadly, I've seen beginner MLLs at the back of the room on a computer game or even coloring mindlessly, and that's not at all what we want. Although many newcomers go through a silent period, that doesn't mean they can't participate in our classrooms. Even just listening and soaking up the classroom culture is learning! Think of how tiring it would be to be in a new space and experiencing a new language.

Our job as educators, at all levels, no matter what we teach, is to figure out ways to engage all our students. We need to find a way to scaffold their learning to include them in the grade-level education curriculum. All too often, I hear from content teachers, *This child just can't learn grade level work. They need to be out of my classroom and work exclusively with the language teacher.* This may be a preference because teaching a newcomer MLL may be a new experience, and we may be mainly underprepared to find a way forward. However, the perception that a beginner MLL cannot access grade level content is inaccurate. Content teachers at all levels can find ways for beginning MLLs to participate, especially since it's not enough for language support to only happen during the part of the day or week that the students are with the language specialist. It may look different, it may sound different, and it will likely require more thought and preparation than we are used to. It's imperative that we change our mindsets and practices to meet the needs of our diverse learners. If we don't find a way to include these students in our classroom community, then how are we fulfilling the vision of education?

How do we do this? More than anything, if you have an MLL specialist to work with, please utilize that person to help build your capacity to reach and teach your language learners. It's not enough for the MLL specialist to provide his or her instruction for the part of the day when he or she works with your MLLs, whether that time is in your classroom or outside of your classroom in a separate setting. It's essential that MLLs get access to meaningful and language-rich instruction all day. If you follow the suggestions presented in this guide that give you a language lens, as many content teachers I've worked with have, your practice can improve to be more equitable for your MLLs and your ALLs. And if you need more help, please keep trying and reach out to colleagues for support.

A. Create tiered assignments

When our classrooms have different proficiency levels, we can provide slightly different assignments to different groups or individuals to meet them at their challenge zone. Let's say we are teaching story elements in language arts. For beginning MLLs, we can provide a graphic organizer with icons for each section: *who/characters, where/setting, first event, second event,* and *third event*. For intermediate and advanced MLLs, we might remove some of this scaffolding and not use icons at all but just list characters, setting, and events. However, we are baking in *accommodations* to *amplify language,* not *water down* the content standards! See the section below on "making over" tasks below, plus related resources available at languagelens.com in the data and assessment category.

B. Pre-teach key content and go beyond pull-out or separate language instruction only

If you're a content teacher lucky enough to have a language specialist to work with, please utilize this person's talents to benefit your students. One key way of using the MLL teacher is to share what's coming ahead in the school year so that he or she can be proactive in setting cohesive goals for your shared students. As discussed earlier, we want to break down the silos of *my kids* and *your kids*; we want language specialists and content specialists to work together to meet common goals for our students. *Pre-teaching* or *frontloading* is a pro tip; giving students some key information and language in advance of whole group instruction gives them additional time and repetition and more opportunities to learn in a new language. I've worked with teachers who provide frontloaded information for ALL students through a quick video preview (especially during the pandemic!) or flipped classroom model. Excellent thinking!

C. Be Intentional about Your Instructional Language

When we teach, we broadcast a message. We want that message to be comprehensible to students. When we broadcast our message, we expect students to interpret it through their input channels of listening and/or reading. We also want them to interact with the message so they can process it and learn it through the output channels of speaking and/or writing. Here we will focus on first listening, then reading scaffolds.

Be aware of the rate of speech you use when instructing. Let's start by talking about our talking. The sheer fact is that many of us, as teachers, talk really fast. I know I'm guilty of it and need to check myself. We also may mumble and string keywords together in what linguists call connected speech so that all the words stick together, like *Howzitgoin?* or *The oppozitofupisdown*. A student listening to these sentences may hear the word *zit* when it's actually not a word spoken here. We blur words and phrases together in speech, and while that's how language works and how we want our students to speak as they become proficient, we don't want our speech to be a barrier to learning.

Be aware of the amount of speech you use when instructing. Another factor in our speech is the sheer amount of language we use. While we don't want to water down our instruction, we do want to use our speech as an instructional modality, not overpower students' auditory processing with too much information at once or unrelated information. For instance:

> *When you get in groups, first, assign roles. Then, oh wait, that reminds me that last week we ran out of the notecards for the reporters in each group. I forgot to go to the office supply cabinet downstairs, so let me write myself a quick note to do that. Anyway, then, read the chapter, which I think you'll love because it's about dogs, and we've been studying the Iditarod, plus many of you have pets.*

You may notice here that a lot is going on in the example above. Rephrasing or even repeating the language can be helpful, but going off on tangents can be very confusing because students may not know what they are—and aren't— supposed to pay deep attention to. Also, if we are giving directions, let's *chunk and chew* multiple steps so students can follow along. I like to use my fingers as a nonverbal tool — First, Next, and Then— to indicate separate steps. I also like to have students (or adult learners!) paraphrase the directions to make sure they really understand the process ahead. Instructional language can be just as complex as the academic language in the task! So use the language lens accordingly when speaking, including the amount of speech you're using. Can you say less with more?

Be aware of the expressions, or idioms, you use when instructing. It's incredible how many cultural expressions and idioms are embedded within our language. I encourage teachers to reflect on what they hear come out of their own mouths that may be completely confusing for language learners if they haven't heard this expression before. For example:

- *Every cloud has a silver lining*
- *Get your act together*
- *On the ball*
- *Speak of the devil*
- *Rocket science*
- *Cut corners*

Reflect on these and ask yourself, *Do these expressions literally make sense?* The answer is no; they all have figurative meanings. Idioms are very culturally loaded, so while some do cross languages, many do not. I am not suggesting not using them at all because they are very important parts of our vernacular. I am simply suggesting that you use your language lens to use them with care and purpose, knowing that language cannot be separated from culture.

D. Make learning goals and success criteria explicit for students.

As I shared in Chapter 3, the importance of making language visible to language learners cannot be understated. MLLs and ALLs benefit from a clear purpose for learning so they know what's coming and how to see if they made the target. Sometimes I walk into a classroom, and it's really unclear what is happening. Students seem unclear, as evidenced by off-task behavior or general looks of confusion. More than anything, one can see a discrepancy between what is taught and what is learned when the data show it. If an assessment is given and students don't demonstrate the expected knowledge and skills, the instruction is often to blame, not the students. Ask yourself the following questions:

- Do I make the goals of the unit clear for students?
- Is this task's language clear and supported through scaffolds for students?
- Do students know what success looks like in each assignment?
- Do I have checks along the way for students to show they are on track?
- Do I consistently refer back to the standards and reteach as necessary?

Success criteria means getting clear on what success looks like, or *when* we *are successful, so* students are clear on what the teacher uses to show mastery (Hattie, 2023, p. 313). If I were to put forth success criteria for you in this learning journey, I'd say that I'd like you to speak and write about what practices in this guide you found useful, what practices you were already doing, and what practices you'd like to try. Ultimately, I want you to transfer this learning to actual behaviors in your classroom. If you needed to write a response for me to show me what you learned from this guidebook, I'd look for something like this, which could be an exemplar of sorts:

This guide validates much of what I already knew about supporting my language learners in my classroom, and it also provides some new ideas I hadn't thought of before. For example, I was reminded that getting to know students is critical, and so is collaborating with my MLL specialist at my school. Yet I also discovered that all my students are language learners, *so using a language lens is something I want to do to benefit my MLLs and my ALLs. Specific things I'd like to try include doing a student data dive for some students that I've had a hard time getting to know, making sure I use all four language domains in every lesson, and trying out some new vocabulary teaching like academic language journals and TPR. I already feel like I can do this!*

Here I've given you an example of how I would set you up for success in a learning experience by using clear targets and success criteria. I also want to stress how important the supports, or scaffolds, along the way are, too. The guide is full of supports like graphics, examples, text features, and the like! As I've done here, I encourage you to consistently plan for these key parts of your lessons so students know what is expected and that they have met the intended outcomes. More than anything, an equity-based mindset is critical so that, as I've modeled for you above, any learner starts with what they bring to the table and constructs new learning from there.

Throughout this guide, I've encouraged you to write out your success criteria—the exact language—you'd want students to use to the learning target for any given assignment. If we do that here for you based on the response above, we could then create a paragraph frame (with sentence frames inside!) like this:

> [Introductory sentence with a claim] This guide validates ____________, and it also ____________. [Cite evidence #1] For example, I was reminded that __________ is critical, [Cite evidence #2] so is __________. [Cite evidence #3] Yet I also discovered that ______________, so using a language lens is something I want to do to

benefit my __________. [Share your next steps here] Specific things I'd like to try include __________, __________ and __________. [Add your own concluding sentence here]

As you can see in this above paragraph frame, I've used an example of what I'd like to read if you, the reader, were to write a claim-based argument that *identifies* effective practices that you have *analyzed* throughout your reading! Bonus if you add the page numbers to support your text-based evidence. I've added cues in this paragraph frame (also referred to as cloze) to help you construct your writing. If this book were in color, I could use color coding strategically. As I shared in the above section on tiering assignments, some learners may not need this scaffold. However, some might! I find that scripting an example of a successful response really helps us see what needs to be clarified and more supported for our students. Do you see through your language lens how you can do this same process for your students? In my classroom, I used this strategy verbally so that students had to fill-the-blank of what I was saying. It is a great way to check for understanding and even gamify learning!

E. Connect speech to text by posting anchor charts or key words and phrases.

One important way of making speech more comprehensible for students is connecting print, or text, to oral language as much as possible. To use the earlier example of the teacher giving a task for reading about the Iditarod, I recommend posting a numbered list of the tasks. I would also have student tools in the groups for the roles expected as they read, including key sentence frames for discussion (e.g., *This paragraph is about_______. I agree with _________because in the text is says______ on page ____*). By making instructional language visible, we are giving our language learners more of an opportunity to be successful as they learn new content.

To connect speech to content-related text, a common strategy that can work in K–12 is the explicit use of *anchor charts*. Anchor charts are posters co-created by the teacher and students to make content more comprehensible. They can also be created on slides online or with other tech tools. Remember that when hearing new language, learners need to see it and hopefully read and write it. It takes multiple exposures and meaningful uses to really learn a new word for any learner. MLLs need even more context, repetition, and connection across the domains. Plus, our ALLs benefit!

F. Choose diverse texts.

In Chapter 2, I underscored the importance of honoring students' experiences and incorporating them into the classroom as mirrors of their identities. By texts, I mean literature, math story problems, artwork, music, and videos. Virtually any source we use is a text of sorts. A helpful way of thinking about how accessible our texts are for our students is thinking of them as either *windows* or *mirrors* (Style, 1996). *Mirrors* are essentially texts in which students can see parts of their identities reflected, *windows* are when we learn about a new perspective, and *sliding glass doors* are somewhere in between.

We want students to know how to find access points into the texts we teach. Invite students to share their perspectives as they relate, or don't relate, to the text you're using. Don't assume that every student in the class can or can't relate. Some students may want to share their perspectives; some may not, and they shouldn't be forced to do so. You can model for them how to use the concept of windows and mirrors by sharing some of your experiences at your comfort level. Some schools I work with find this concept very useful for their students and their library. They audit their book lists and other sets of texts (video, art, music) to see if they have a disproportionate number of mirrors or windows based on the diversity of their student population and how their unique student body comprised of individuals identify themselves.

G. Supplement and amplify texts.

Just using the grade level textbook as the sole text for teaching content isn't enough; students need multiple modalities and often varying reading levels to access meaning. Supplemental texts can really help enrich a unit. Look for news articles, magazine pictures, videos, and fiction and nonfiction examples of the topic to bring the world into the classroom and raise interest levels. Amplify the grade-level text or even texts beyond the grade level by annotating with students and even rewriting the text at a more accessible level and format with lots of text features. A lot of teachers I know work in teams of MLL specialists and content teachers to rewrite, what I like to call *amplify,* textbook excerpts at a more student-friendly reading level without simplifying the message.

Like the makeover process explained more in depth below, add visuals and other student tools like reading response areas for students to stop-and-jot their ideas, connections, and questions along the way. When educators take the time to both supplement and amplify texts for students at all proficiency levels, they can use these materials year after year, adding to their resources to stay relevant and keep students interested in the content. As I keep saying, don't reinvent the wheel! Simply adjust, align, and refine as needed for students that come your way through the years.

H. Use mentor texts and anchor papers for students to use in writing and speaking.

If we want students to talk and write like scholars, then we need them to see and hear examples. As you read in this guidebook time and time again, mentor texts or exemplars can be used to show students what the target language sounds like and looks like in your content area. Mentor texts can be right from an expert in the field, and they can also be created by the teacher and/or students themselves, which may also be called *anchor papers.*

One teacher I worked with implemented academic conversations across his social studies lessons on climate change. Then he taught students how to take what they were saying in their oral discourse and put it on paper. That way, their writing was intentionally linked to their oral language and vice versa. He had been showing them mentor texts of how sociologists wrote about climate change, but his students couldn't seem to make the connection to make their writing *sound like a sociologist* reporting on this topic until he had them connect their speaking to their writing using specific content phrases. For example, *Given the need to search for climate change solutions, we need to explore alternative energies.* This is certainly not a simple sentence! Yet if we were to make it one, it could sound like this: *Scientists need to find more energy solutions to address climate change.* Creating these complex sentences isn't necessarily easy for any language learner, so by deconstructing the language used under the guidance of a teacher like this one here, students can see how to create their own academic language versions themselves.

I. Reduce cultural and linguistic bias through a task makeover

Many content teachers I work with learn about providing more access to MLLs and ALLs in their instruction, only to discover that their everyday tasks and assessments also need a makeover. *Who doesn't love a makeover?* Many times, our summative assessment tasks and formative assessment assignments are not designed as accessibly as they could be for our learners. In other words, they aren't always a valid measure of learning. How do we make sure our assessments are more valid? The answer is that we need to use our language lens to minimize what we can of barriers or biases, in terms of language and culture.

Linguistic bias happens when language doesn't allow students to show what they know accurately. Many tasks become a language test instead of a test on how students can recall or use concepts in a content area.

Cultural bias occurs when the topics within a task are not topics or situations a student can relate to, thus thwarting the validity of the assessment because it was likely not designed with a multicultural perspective or through the multiple perspectives of learners in front of us.

For instance, a state test I gave my fourth graders had students read about some children who loved their treehouse. It asked them multiple-choice questions about the most likely reason the students liked the treehouse. This assessment was problematic for several reasons. First, the topic was a treehouse, and my students lived in the inner city with few trees, with gang violence outside—including periodic gunshots on the street—and certainly no treehouses. The students could not relate to the story's premise, and many were very confused about why there would ever be a house in a tree in the first place. Therefore, in my view, this was a culturally biased text. It wasn't just texting reading skills, it was testing culture. It came from a specific socio-economic and even racial perspective that did not include my students.

Second, the language used in the questions was linguistically tricky. The term most likely, it can be argued, for many MLLs and even for ALLs can transpose itself to seem to mean like the most. We don't necessarily use the term most likely in everyday instruction or social language, yet large-scale assessments are often over-reliant on this kind of complex instructional language, which can become linguistically biased in cases where students don't have experience with this kind of language. Now, you might be thinking, *But can't we teach to the test?* Instead, the question could be: *How can we promote authentic assessment opportunities in our classrooms to provide evidence beyond the large-scale big data?* Or: *How can our students demonstrate content-area knowledge in various ways, often in ways that are more meaningful and connected to the real world?*

J. Use descriptive feedback on growth as part of a holistic assessment model

It cannot be stated strongly enough how important it is to use specific feedback when supporting students, not just general praise like *Good job!* or *You're smart!* Students need a safe classroom environment in which to take risks where information is shared with them about how their efforts are helping—or not helping—them reach the intended learning goals (Wiggins, Wiliam, Tovani, Johnston Chappuis,, Hattie & Brookhart, 2012). In fact, effective instruction incorporates consistent feedback to students on their growth, also known as *formative assessment*.

In reflecting on this practice, I recommend first taking a look at the language— including body language—you use with students. Make eye contact and smile, if that's your style, to encourage students and let them know you care. However, keep in mind that not all cultures view eye contact the same way, so some students may not make eye contact back, and that doesn't necessarily mean they don't respect you. Nodding to show you understand and noticing when students put forth effort, even if it's not the same kind of effort as other students, is important so that all students feel included as part of the learning community. More than anything, demonstrating a growth mindset (Dweck, 2016) through your language and overall tone is imperative. Students can shut down if they get an inkling that we don't believe they can do it. Plus, I cannot understate the importance of *wait time* or giving students a chance to deeply process before responding. Make this practice a part of class discussions, group work, and one-on-one feedback sessions.

The language you use in your formative assessments matters for written and verbal feedback. Use pointed data to share the next steps and encourage student construction of goals going forward. When working one-on-one, instead of *Nice work*! try, *You wrote the word grand here. I can see that you thought it would be a stronger word here than good, which we've talked about as a goal for your writing. Nice work taking that extra step to improve your word choice!* When closing up a lesson with the whole class, instead of It was too loud today during work time. Let's do better tomorrow, try I noticed that four out of five groups were focused on the project while I was working with the fifth group. However, those four groups didn't all seem to be following our protocol in terms of having one student talk at a time. Does anyone have ideas about how we can improve on that tomorrow? Instead of *You didn't spell it right*, try, *You didn't spell it right yet; how can we make sure you remember this tricky word? What do you need to move towards that goal?*

Student self-reflection and peer-reflection go a long way. Remember, we are trying to build independent thinkers and learners, so encouraging students to share feedback on their own learning and share feedback on peers' learning is an important part of the language lens approach. Measuring student progress should be holistic, not solely focused on test scores and quantitative data. Students are fully dimensional, and our assessment should be, too. Often, students, especially MLL students, can be reduced to their large-scale, summative test scores both in content and English language proficiency. One small yet important shift we can make is to focus on development, not just proficiency. Because multilingual learners are acquiring an additional language, let's focus on that growth which is nuanced, fluid, and different across various contexts. How do we do this?

One place to start is to have students simply find a *glow* and a *grow* for their learning. For example, Figure 5.4 gives a sample rubric structure for simple, student-centered goal setting and reflection. Hattie (2023) gives a set of questions: *Where have I done well? Where do I need to improve? How can I improve? What can I do next time?* (p. 339). Let's put the power of measuring growth in students' hands so they can be drivers of their own learning! See the resources for data and assessments at languagelens.com.

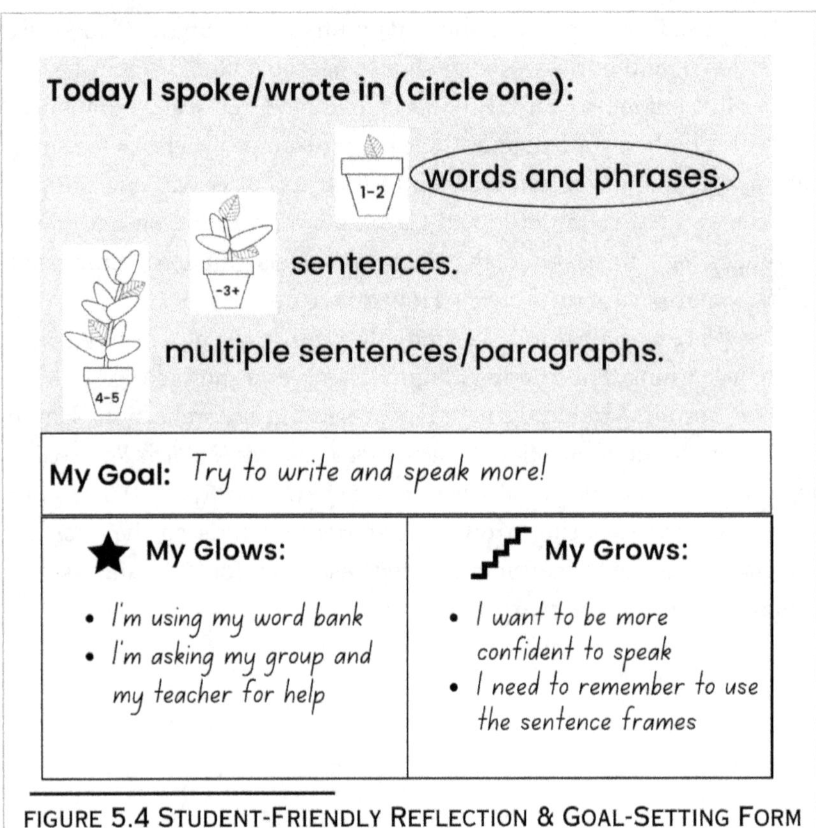

FIGURE 5.4 STUDENT-FRIENDLY REFLECTION & GOAL-SETTING FORM

In Summary

There is a wide variety of scaffolds and activities that can support your content teaching. As you reviewed the ideas in this chapter, you might have found some that you already use and some that you'd like to try. I want to stress that there is no one way to scaffold your teaching. If you're looking to put all the pieces together, I recommend creating your own language lens planning tool or checklist of what you can build into your classroom as *routines* to be sure you're putting into practice what we've explored.

To summarize our journey together, I'll share the gist of this guidebook and how I explained it in a recent interview, "The most important thing that teachers can do to support their multilingual students is to teach their students, not just the content...to start by learning about who the students are, trying to put themselves in students' shoes, leading with empathy and compassion and then really thinking about the tasks, the demands of the lesson with those learners in mind" (Ottow, 2022, as featured in Ellevation Education). Be intentional about your planning, teaching and assessing, enacting *confianza,* mutual respect and trust, between yourself and your students. Learning is a two-way street!

With your language lens, you now know how important it is to consider your own identity as you start with your students from their perspectives. Build student ownership of learning so that students are invested in their own process of learning. Structure your classroom so that students work directly with each other to foster collaborative, meaningful, and interactive discussions. Consistently check for understanding with your students to make sure they are right alongside you in the learning journey. Create thoughtful, authentic assessment opportunities that make learning come alive for students. Learn from your students, too. Consult your language specialist and colleagues whenever possible. Have faith in yourself. Have respect for your students. Overall, understand that teaching is a *practice,* something we are always refining and learning more about. The important thing is that we keep refining our practice in service of our students so that they love learning, too.

~

TIPS FOR TEACHERS: WHAT WILL YOU ADD TO YOUR LANGUAGE LENS TOOLBOX?

1. Which of these scaffolds and activities presented in this chapter do you currently have in your toolbox for all your students? Which of these scaffolds could be added? When and why? Which could become routines, not just one-offs? What do you need to do or prepare to successfully implement these ideas?

• • •

2. In thinking about the specific needs of your students, are there individual students who could benefit from additional scaffolds than the ones you use for your whole class?

3. Are there ways you can collaborate with your content team members, your language specialist, and/or a coach to tighten up the language scaffolds in your content classroom? Here are some ideas to do on your own or with a team:

4. With a colleague, analyze the use of your classroom real estate to see if it maximizes student learning. Consider how students help design the use of the room and ask them for input. For example, students can learn how to separate desks from groups during a whole-group mini-lesson or lecture and then return to groups for group work. Students may also want access to laptops as a learning tool more consistently, with guidelines for use. Students can learn how to change how the room functions and looks and feels to maximize their learning. Utilize the input of colleagues and your students to improve the conditions for learning in your classroom with a language lens.

5. Reflect on a typical lesson by recording yourself or having a colleague or coach observe you to share their feedback. Reflect on your instructional language, including the rate and amount of speech you use, plus clear directions and nonverbals. Note the scaffolding in place or not in place and where it could be more effective. Consider if certain scaffolds are needed for the whole class or if assignments can be tiered for various language needs.

6. Audit your classroom texts to see if they contain windows and/or mirrors of your students' experiences. Analyze what perspectives may be missing and find more texts to add to your collection using your students' and peers' support and collective wisdom.

. . .

7. Give an existing task a makeover by reviewing the tips presented in this chapter and in the additional resources for data and assessments available at languagelens.com. See what little adjustments could be made to make the assessment more accessible to learners, reducing cultural and/ or linguistic bias. Consider what implications this makeover may have for your universal instruction, too. These tips can be brought into any instructional task. They may give you further insight into what barriers need to be removed or reduced to make your instruction and assessment more accessible for your language learners.

8. Go back to the self-assessment in Chapter 1. Retake it. Notice what's different. Do you have any new understandings? New takeaways or next steps? You may want to write about any shifts in thinking, feeling, or thinking with a simple prompt: *I used to...but now....* Choose a few things to try out in your classroom. Celebrate your growth and implement this new learning right away for your students!

TIPS FOR COACHES AND LEADERS: HOW DO WE SUSTAIN AND SCALE SYSTEMIC PRACTICES FOR MAXIMUM IMPACT ACROSS OUR SCHOOL?

1. As instructional leaders, our focus is human capital development. Just like we ask teachers to monitor students' progress, we must support educators on our "caseload" through ongoing progress monitoring as well. How are you currently being visible in your school, in the classrooms? Do you know where individual educators are along the continuum of teacher development? How about your teams? Some may be proficient/ advanced, at a more advanced 2.0 level, whereas others may need a lot more direction to set goals because they are still working on foundational aspects of teaching and learning, or a 1.0 level, as I like to say. Plan your schedule for support accordingly and

work closely with your instructional leadership team to monitor educators' growth.

2. In order to sustain and scale the language lens in your school, I recommend thinking beyond one classroom to the entire school. We can make systemic change when we focus on the system, not just individuals. Focus brings people together towards one goal. For example, let me tell you about a high school leader I coached. When we did diagnostic learning walks together, we found that students were not speaking in complete sentences. We also analyzed multiple measures of student test scores that showed writing was an area needing improvement schoolwide. However, we know the connection between speaking and writing, so we decided to focus on getting students to engage more through extended discourse so that they could transfer speaking to listening. We did this in a very systematic way. We built the capacity of the teaching staff by showing them the data we collected of how many times we heard students in words versus how many times we heard students speak in complete sentences. We asked every teacher to make sure students answered questions in complete sentences. The principal and the coach led workshops on building student discourse and academic conversation strategies. The school created a student self-assessment rubric for students to self-assess and peer assess their language production so students could clearly see the success criteria. Through this shared vision and toolkit, the cognitive load, or the amount of memory a brain can hold at one time, was lowered. Teachers' cognitive load was lowered because they had a shared language and a shared set of methods to implement in their classrooms and analyze the effects of in their common planning time. Students' cognitive load was lowered because the same strategies and expectations were clear in all of their classrooms and, over time, multiple measures of data showed their growth in speaking and writing! Too often, across a school, teachers across departments and/or different grade levels compete for students' brain space with different expectations and strategies. As leaders, we can create focus and cohesion by having schoolwide processes that yield positive systemic

change. How can you focus your systemic change on schoolwide practices? How can you lead a shared, schoolwide language and a shared, schoolwide toolkit?

3. If you value time to support educators, how is that time reflected in your weekly schedule? Are you scheduling in time to check for understanding of teachers' goals through an ongoing observation/coaching schedule? For those who need less support, perhaps you are planning for a simple check-in occasionally. For those who need more support, I recommend ensuring they get actual coaching cycles, not just a check-in. A coaching cycle is a process that typically consists of a pre-observation conference to learn about what you'll observe and to help the educator set their goal for the observation. The next step is typically the observation, where the coach/leader carefully tracks real-time classroom coaching data. I recommend tracking data based on what the teacher or teaching team asked you to look for. I also recommend looking out for other coachable moments like mapping out interactions, tallying who is on/off task, noticing disproportionalities in equity of voice, use of instructional time, and classroom management, just to mention a few. What I tell coaches and leaders when I train them to coach through a language lens is that it is not about looking for everything at once but widening the aperture of your language lens to attune to the areas that need the most attention now on behalf of students on the margins.

4. Look inward at your school culture. Asset map the classrooms where the language lens is working. Notice where the needs are. Continuously bring your leadership team to take advantage of embedded professional learning spaces to reinforce essential practices you want to see in all classrooms as part of your vision of equitable instruction for your students. For example, if the co-planning, co-teaching, and co-assessing with a language lens is a goal of your school, notice where that's working in classrooms and collect artifacts of practice. Give shout-outs to teams working and reworking their student-centered

collaborative norms. Have other teams visit those co-planning sessions and co-teaching in action. Focus on the impact of teacher development on student learning. I call this embedded professional learning of peer coaching *showcasing*. Feel free to look through the principles for professional learning on our website at Confianza to reflect on how you/your team approaches professional learning at your school: ellstudents.com/research-base

5. Foster a *culture of learning* not a culture of competition. Leverage the role of teacher leaders and coaches to be these conduits of matching educators based on assets and needs in a non-evaluative way! Coaches can help schedule and facilitate peer observations with focused debrief sessions. Coaches can help cultivate this culture of learning by facilitating consultancies and bringing in protocols to analyze student work consistently and in all teams. Just like we want to foster student agency, we also want to foster educator agency. This is the most important parallel practice of all, in my opinion, to sustain and scale effective practice on behalf of our students. Have teachers share, support and lead!

REFERENCES

Adger, C., Snow, C., & Christian, D. (2018). *What Teachers Need to Know about Language* (2nd ed.). Washington, DC: Multilingual Matters.

Ahmed, S. K. (2018). *Being the Change: Lessons and Strategies to Teach Social Comprehension*. Portsmouth, NH: Heinemann.

Bailey, A. L. & Huang, B. H. (2011). Do Current English Language Development/Proficiency Standards Reflect the English Needed for Success in School? *Language Testing*, 28, 343–65. https://journals.sagepub.com/doi/abs/10.1177/0265532211404187?journalCode=ltja

Baker, C. (2014). *A Parents' and Teachers' Guide to Bilingualism* (4th ed.). Tonawanda, NY: Multilingual Matters.

Bear, C., & McEvoy, J. (2015, June 9). In California Schools, Thousands of English Language Learners Getting Stuck. *KQED*. https://www.kqed.org/news/10552284/in-california-schools-thousands-of-english-language-learners-getting-stuck

Beard, R. (2018). How to Pronounce GHOTI. *Alpha Dictionary*. https://www.alphadictionary.com/articles/ling006.html

Bellamy, C. (2022, July 22). Henry Louis Gates Jr. Announced as Editor-in-Chief of the New Oxford Dictionary of African American English. *NBC News*. https://www.nbcnews.com/news/nbcblk/henry-louis-gates-jr-announced-editor-chief-new-oxford-dictionary-afri-rcna39554

Baumer, N. and Frueh, J. (2021). What is Neurodiversity? *Harvard Health Publishing: Harvard Medical School*. https://www.health.harvard.edu/blog/what-is-neurodiversity-202111232645

BlackDeer, Dr. (@drblackdeer). "If I'm not mistaken, every culture has some way of saying "mind your business"...Let's share some of our faves below to help those boundary-challenged folx in our lives get the message." October, 22, 2022, 5:18PM. https://twitter.com/DrBlackDeer/status/1583930770569035777?s=20

Brown, A. M. (2017). *Emergent Strategy: Shaping Change, Shaping Worlds*. Chico: AK Press.

Calderon, M. (2007). *Teaching Reading to English Language Learners: Grades 6–12*. Thousand Oaks, CA: Corwin Press.

Canto, M. (2023, March 19). *Commentary: Being multilingual is no longer a liability for students. That's good for the U.S.* Los Angeles Times. https://www.latimes.com/opinion/story/2023-03-19/la-ed-bilingualism-superpower

Centers for Disease Control and Prevention. (2020). *Disability and Health Overview*. https://www.cdc.gov/ncbddd/disabilityandhealth/disability.html

Centers for Disease Control and Prevention. (2021, August 14). *Hospitalization Rates and Characteristics of Children Aged <18 Years Hospitalized with Laboratory-Confirmed COVID-19 — COVID-NET, 14 States, March 1–July 25, 2020*. https://www.cdc.gov/mmwr/volumes/69/wr/mm6932e3.htm?s

Cochran-Smith, M. and Lytle, S. (2009). *Inquiry as Stance: Practitioner Research for the Next Generation*. New York: Teachers College Press.

Colorin Colorado. (2017). *Using Cognates to Develop Comprehension in English.* http://www.colorincolorado.org/article/using-cognates-develop-comprehension-english

Confianza. (2018). *Empowering Teachers through Confianza's Action Cycle.* https://vimeo.com/videos/278226343

Commission on Language Learning at the American Academy of Arts and Sciences (n.d.). *The State of Languages in the U.S.: A Statistical Portrait.* Cambridge, MA: American Academy of Arts and Sciences. https://www.amacad.org/sites/default/files/academy/multimedia/pdfs/publications/researchpapersmonographs/State-of-Languages-in-US.pdf

Council of Chief State School Officers. (2023, April). *English Language Proficiency (ELD) Standards.* Council of Chief State School Officers. https://ccsso.org/resource-library/english-language-proficiency-elp-standards

Coxhead, A. (n.d.) The Academic Word List. *Victoria University of Wellington, New Zealand.* https://www.wgtn.ac.nz/lals/resources/academicwordlist

Cummins, J. (2010). The Three Pillars of English Language Learning. *RITMLL.* https://www.ritell.net/Resources/Documents/General%20Education%20Resources/the%20three%20pillars%20of%20english%20language%20learning%20(1).pdf

Cummins, J., Bismilla, V., Chow, P., Cohen, S., Giampapa, F., Leoni, L., Sandhu, P. & Sastri, P. (2005, September). Affirming Identity in Multilingual Classrooms. *Educational Leadership, 63* (1). https://files.ascd.org/staticfiles/ascd/pdf/journals/ed_lead/el200509_cummins.pdf

Cummins, J. (2017) Teaching Minoritized Students: Are Additive Approaches Legitimate? *Harvard Educational Review, 87* (3), 404-425). https://www.cpatrickproctor.com/uploads/9/0/9/1/9091150/cummins_2017.pdf

DeCapua, A. & Marshall, Tang, H.W. (2020) *Meeting the Needs of SLIFE: A Guide for Educators, 2nd Edition.* University of Michigan Press.

Duguay, A., Massoud, L., Tabuka, L., Himmel, J. & Sugarman, J. (2013). Implementing the Common Core for English Learners. *CAL Practitioner Brief.* http://www.cal.org/siop/pdfs/briefs/implementing-common-core-for-english-learners.pdf

Duke, N. (2016). What Doesn't Work: Literacy Practices We Should Abandon. *Edutopia.* https://www.edutopia.org/blog/literacy-practices-we-should-abandon-nell-k-duke

Durham, A. (2023, March 30). Educators respond: Designing professional learning when teachers are overwhelmed. *Learning Forward.* https://learningforward.org/2023/03/30/professional-learning-for-tired-teachers/

Dutro, S., & Kinsella, K. (2010). English Language Development: Issues and Implementation at Grades Six through Twelve. In *Center for Applied Linguistics: Improving Education for English Learners: Research-Based Approaches.* CA: Hippocrene Books.

Dweck, C. (2016). *Mind-Set: The New Psychology of Success.* New York: Penguin Random House.

Ebbers, S. (2008). Linking the Language: A Cross-Disciplinary Vocabulary Approach. *Reading Rockets.* https://www.readingrockets.org/article/linking-language-cross-disciplinary-vocabulary-approach

Echevarria, J., Short, D., & Powers, K. (2006). School Reform and Standards-Based Education: An Instructional Model for English Language Learners. *Journal of Educational Research, 99* (4), 195–210.

Echevarria, J., Vogt, M. E., & Short, D. (2017). *Making Content Comprehensible for English Learners: The SIOP® Model* (5th ed.). Boston: Allyn & Bacon.

Ellevation Education (2023). Supporting Long-Term English Learners: Start by Changing the Label. https://ellevationeducation.com/supporting-LTELs-changing-the-label

Ellis, R. (n.d.). Teaching an English Learner who is Deafblind. *Paths to Literacy*. https://www.pathstoliteracy.org/teaching-english-learner-who-deafblind/

English Learner Success Forum. (2022). New National Research Raises Teacher Voices about Instructional Materials for English Learners. https://www.elsuccessforum.org/blog/new-national-research-raises-teachers-voices-about-instructional-materials-for-english-learners

Essberger, J. (2018). Ghoti = Fish. *English Club*. https://www.englishclub.com/esl-articles/199909.htm

Florida, R. (2017). Without Immigrants, the Fortune 500 Would be the Fortune 284. *Center for American Entrepreneurship*. https://startupsusa.org/cae-news/without-immigrants-fortune-500-fortune-284/

Freeman, D. & Freeman, Y. (2004). Three Types of English Language Learners. *National Council of Teachers of English*, *9* (4), 1–3.

Freeman, Y., Freeman, D., & Mercuri, S. (2002). *Closing the Achievement Gap: How to Reach Limited-Formal-Schooling and Long-Term English Learners*. Portsmouth, NH: Heinemann.

Fry, R. (2014). U.S. High School Dropout Rate Reaches Record Low, Drive by Improvement Among Hispanics, Blacks. *PEW Research Center*. https://www.pewresearch.org/short-reads/2014/10/02/u-s-high-school-dropout-rate-reaches-record-low-driven-by-improvements-among-hispanics-blacks/

García, D. (2018). Dual Language Series Part I: Who Are Our Learners? *Confianza*. https://ellstudents.com/blogs/the-confianza-way/dual-language-series-part-1

Gee, J. P. (2008). A sociocultural perspective on opportunity to learn. In P. A. Moss, D. C. Pullin, J. P. Gee, E. H. Haertel, & L. J. Young (Eds.), *Assessment, equity, and opportunity to learn*, (p. 76–108). Cambridge University Press.

Gerner de Garica, B. (2013). Who are English Learners with Disabilities? *Impact: Institute on Community Integration*. https://publications.ici.umn.edu/impact/26-1/issues-in-the-education-of-deaf-and-hard-of-hearing-k-12-english-language-learners

Gibbons, P. (2002). *Scaffolding Language, Scaffolding Learning: Teaching Second Language Learners in the Mainstream Classroom*. Portsmouth, NH: Heinemann.

Global Citizen. (2018). Seventeen Famous Immigrants Who Helped Shape America. https://www.globalcitizen.org/en/content/bet-you-didnt-know-these-game-changers-were-immigr

González, N., Moll, L. & Amanti, C. (2005). *Funds of Knowledge: Theorizing Practices in Households, Communities and Classrooms*. Mahwah, NJ: Erlbaum.

Grosjean, F. (2016). What Is Translanguaging? An Interview with Ofelia García. *Psychology Today*. https://www.psychologytoday.com/us/blog/life-bilingual/201603/what-is-translanguaging

Halliday, M. A. K. & Hasan, R. (1989). *Language, Context, and Text*. Oxford, UK: Oxford University Press.

Halliday, M. & Matthiessen, C. (1961). What Is Systemic-Functional Linguistics? *Informa-*

tion on Systemic Functional Linguistics: ISFLA. http://www.isfla.org/Systemics/definition.html

Hammond, Z. (2015). *Culturally Responsive Teaching and the Brain: Promoting Authentic Engagement and Rigor Among Culturally and Linguistically Diverse Students.* Thousand Oaks, CA: Corwin.

Hattie, J. (2023). *Visible Learning: The Sequel, A Synthesis of Over 2, 100 Meta-Analyses Relating to Achievement.* London and New York: Routledge.

Heritage, M., Walqui, A & Linquanti, R. (2015). *English Language Learners and the New Standards: Developing Language, Content Knowledge, and Analytical Practices in the Classroom.* Cambridge, MA: Harvard Education Press.

Honigsfeld, A. & Dove, M. (2019) *Collaborating for English Learners: A Foundational Guide to Integrated Practices (Second Edition).* Thousand Oaks, CA: Corwin Press.

Kopf, D. (2017). The U.S. Has More Immigrant Inventors than Every Other Country Combined. *Quartz.* https://qz.com/890943/the-us-has-more-immigrant-inventors-than-every-other-country-combined/

Krashen, S. & Crawford, J. (2015). *English Learners in American Classrooms: 101 Questions and 101 Answers.* Portland, OR: Diversity Learning K–12.

Leland, A. (2020). Deafblind Communities May be Creating a New Language of Touch. *The New Yorker.* https://www.newyorker.com/culture/annals-of-inquiry/deafblind-communities-may-be-creating-a-new-language-of-touch

Lesaux, N., Galloway, E., & Marietta, S. (2016). *Teaching Advanced Literacy Skills: A Guide for Leaders in Linguistically Diverse Schools.* New York, NY: Guilford Press.

Little, D., Dam, L. & Legenhausen L. (2017). *Language Learner Autonomy: Theory, Practice and Research.* Bristol: Multilingual Matters.

Martinez, C. (2022). Disability Statistics in the U.S.: Looking Beyond Figures for an Accessible and Inclusive Society. *Inclusive City Maker.* https://www.inclusivecitymaker.com/disability-statistics-in-the-us/

McLeod, S. (2018). The Zone of Proximal Development and Scaffolding. *Simply Psychology.* https://www.simplypsychology.org/Zone-of-Proximal-Development.html

McTighe, J. & Wiggins, G. (2012). Understanding by Design Framework. *ASCD.* https://www.ascd.org/ASCD/pdf/siteASCD/publications/UbD_WhitePaper0312.pdf

Moll, L. (1992). Funds of Knowledge for Teaching: Using a Qualitative Approach to Connect Homes and Classrooms. *Theory into Practice, 31*(2), 132–41.

Muhammad, G. (2020) *Cultivating Genius: An Equity Framework for Culturally and Historically Responsive Literacy.* New York: Scholastic.

National Council on Teacher Quality (2015). *Teacher Prep Review: A Review of the Nation's Teacher Preparatory Programs.* https://www.nctq.org/dmsView/Teacher_Prep_Review_2014_Report

National Center for Educational Statistics (2022). *English Learners in Public Schools.* https://nces.ed.gov/programs/coe/indicator/cgf

Nora, J., & Echevarria, J. (2016). *No More Low Expectations for English Learners.* Portsmouth, NH: Heinemann.

Otheguy, R., García, O., & Reid, W. (2015). Clarifying Translanguaging and Deconstructing Named Languages: A Perspective from Linguistics. *Applied Linguistics Review, 6* (3): 281–307.

Ottow, S. & Holmes, J. (2014). *Improved Student Learning through Teacher Inquiry.* MATSOL Currents. https://www.matsol.org/assets/documents/currentsv37no1springsummer2014.pdf

Ottow, S. (2015). The Problem with PD: Redefine and Reconceptualize the Power of Professional Learning. *Confianza.* https://ellstudents.com/blogs/the-confianza-way/the-problem-with-pd

Ottow, S. (2018). *Equity, Language, and Literacy:* Harvard Graduate School of Education EL Summit. https://vimeo.com/258261385

Ottow, S. (2022). Strengthening communication at the sentence level [E-learning module video]. In *Develop Academic Language with Strong Sentences* [E-learning module]. Ellevation Education. https://ellevationeducation.com/product/ellevation-strategies/default

Ovando, C., & Combs, M. C. (2012). *Bilingual and ESL Classrooms: Teaching in Multicultural Contexts.* New York: McGraw-Hill.

PEW. (2014). *Changing Patterns in U.S. Immigration and Population.* http://www.pewtrusts.org/en/research-and-analysis/issue-briefs/2014/12/changing-patterns-in-us-immigration-and-population#0-overview

Pofeldt, E. (2013). First Generation Immigrants Dive into Entrepreneurship. *Forbes.* https://www.forbes.com/sites/elainepofeldt/2013/06/26/first-generation-immigrants-dive-into-entrepreneurship/#7838213774d8

Pollack, M. (2017) *Schooltalk: Rethinking What We Say About—and to—Students Every Day.* New York: The New Press.

Quintero, D., & Hansen, M. (2017). English Learners and the Growing Need for Qualified Teachers. *Brookings Institute.* https://www.brookings.edu/blog/brown-center-chalkboard/2017/06/02/english-learners-and-the-growing-need-for-qualified-teachers/

Ravishankar, R.A. (2020). *Why You Need to Stop Using These Words and Phrases. Ascend: Harvard Business Review.* https://hbr.org/2020/12/why-you-need-to-stop-using-these-words-and-phrases

Reading Rockets (2019). *Accommodations and Modifications.* https://www.readingrockets.org/article/accommodations-and-modifications

Rehn, A. (2016). The 20-Minute Rule for Great Public Speaking: On Attention Spans and Keeping Focus. *The Art of Keynoting.* https://medium.com/the-art-of- keynoting/the-20-minute-rule-for-great-public-speaking-on-attention-spans-and-keeping-focus-7370cf06b636

Rymer, R. (2012, July) *Vanishing Voices.* National Geographic. https://www.nationalgeographic.com/magazine/article/vanishing-languages

Rosa, J. & Flores, N. (2021). Decolonization, Language, and Race in Applied Linguistics and Social Justice. *Oxford University Press.* https://academic.oup.com/applij/article-abstract/42/6/1162/6484970

Said, S. (2023). Techquity Post-Covid Requires A Social Emotional Learning Lens Part 2. *Confianza.* https://ellstudents.com/blogs/the-confianza-way/techquity-post-COVID-requires-a-social-emotional-learning-lens-part-2

Salva, C. & Matis, A. (2017). *Boosting Achievement: Reaching Students with Interrupted and Minimal Education.* Irving, TX: Seidlitz Education.

Samuels, S. (2021, June 15). Dismantling barriers for English Language Learners.

Edutopia. https://www.edutopia.org/article/dismantling-barriers-english-language-learners/

Schmitt, J. & DeCourcy. (2022, December 6). The pandemic has exacerbated a long-standing national shortage of teachers. *The Economic Policy Institute.* https://www.epi.org/publication/shortage-of-teachers/

Schütz, R. (2017). *Stephen Krashen's Theory of Second Language Acquisition.* http://www.sk.com.br/sk-krash.html

Schwartz, Sarah (2022). *Education Week.* The 'Science of Reading' and English Language-Learners: What the Research Says. https://www.edweek.org/teaching-learning/the-science-of-reading-and-english-language-learners-what-the-research-says/2022/04

Sharma, S.A. & Christ, T. (2017). Five steps toward successful culturally relevant text selection and integration. *The Reading Teacher, 71* (3), 295–307.

Shen, D. (2018). Group and Cooperative Learning: Students as Classroom Leaders. *Harvard University: ABLConnect.* https://ablconnect.harvard.edu/group-cooperative-learning-students-classroom-leaders

Shoichet, C. (2023, April 15). Where immigrants come from and where they go after reaching the US. *CNN.* https://www.cnn.com/2023/04/15/us/where-immigrants-come-from-cec/index.html

Sight Word Games. (2013). *Words with the Prefix "Inter."* http://www.sightwordsgame.com/spMLLing/prefixes/inter/

Snow, C. E. & Uccelli, P. (2009). The Challenge of Academic Language. In D. R. Olson & N. Torrance (Eds.), *The Cambridge Handbook of Literacy.* New York: Cambridge University Press.

Spina, C. (2021). *Moving Beyond for Multilingual Learners.* Alexandria: EduMatch Publishing.

Starbucks. (2018). Caramel Macchiato. https://www.starbucks.com/coffee/espresso/caramel-macchiato-beverages

StarTalk. (2017, February 26). *Twenty Immigrant & Refugee Scientists Who Made America Greater: Part One.* https://startalkmedia.com/20-immigrants-refugee-scientists-who-made-america-greater-part-1/

Style, E. (1996). Curriculum as Window and Mirror. *National SEED Project.* https://nationalseedproject.org/Key-SEED-Texts/curriculum-as-window-and-mirror

Temko, E. (2019). Speaking like a Queen. *EzraTemko.* https://ezratemko.com/drag/speaking-like-a-queen/

TESOL. (2006). *TESOL Pre-K–12 English Language Proficiency Standards Framework.* https://www.tesol.org/professional-development/publications-and-research/research-and-standards/standards/

Thompson, I. (2015). Language Families. *AWL: About World Languages.* http://aboutworldlanguages.com/language-families

Turner, C. (2021). Education Pick Miguel Cardona is New to Washington But Not to Classrooms. *NPR.* https://www.npr.org/2021/02/02/962050863/education-pick-miguel-cardona-is-new-to-washington-but-not-to-classrooms

Tyson, K. (2013). No Tears for Tiers: Common Core Tiered Vocabulary Made Simple. *Dokumen.* https://dokumen.tips/documents/no-tears-for-tiers-common-core-tiered-vocabulary-made-simple-notearsfor.html

United States Department of Education. (2018). *Our Nation's English Learners: Characteristics*. https://www2.ed.gov/datastory/el-characteristics/index.html

Usable Knowledge. (2018, April 25). *Linguistically Responsive Teachers: What Mainstream Classroom Teachers Should Know about Teaching English Learners*. Harvard Graduate School of Education. https://www.gse.harvard.edu/news/uk/18/04/linguistically-responsive-teachers

Villalobos, Jessica. (2020). *An Asset-Based Approach to Support ELL Success*. ASCD. https://www.ascd.org/el/articles/an-asset-based-approach-to-support-ell-success

WIDA Consortium. (2013). *RtI2: Developing a Culturally and Linguistically Responsive Approach to Response to Instruction & Intervention for English Language Learners*. Madison, WI: Board of Regents of the University of Wisconsin System, on behalf of the WIDA Consortium. https://wida.wisc.edu/resources/response-instruction-and-intervention-english-language-learners

Wiggins, G., Wiliam, D., Tovani, C., Johnston, P., Chappuis, J., Hattie, J. & Brookhart, S. (2012). EL Takeaways: Things to Remember about Feedback. *Educational Leadership, 70* (1). http://www.ascd.org/ASCD/pdf/journals/ed_lead/el201209_ takeaways.pdf

Will, M. (2020, April 14). Still Mostly White and Female: New Federal Data on the Teaching Profession. *Education Week*. https://www.edweek.org/leadership/still-mostly-white-and-female-new-federal-data-on-the-teaching-profession/2020/04

Zwiers, J. (2014). *Building Academic Language: Meeting Common Core Standards Across Disciplines* (2nd ed.). San Francisco: John Wiley & Sons.

Printed in the USA
CPSIA information can be obtained
at www.ICGtesting.com
LVHW021329191223
766860LV00004B/145